CREATING PROPERTY WEALTH
IN ANY MARKET

PHILIPPE BRACH

First published in 2016 by Major Street Publishing Pty Ltd
Contact: E info@majorstreet.com.au
             M 0421 707 983

© Philippe Brach 2016
The moral rights of the authors have been asserted

National Library of Australia Cataloguing-in-Publication entry
Creator: Brach, Philippe, author
Title: Creating property wealth in any market: how to build a high performance property portfolio / Philippe Brach
ISBN: 978-0-9945452-0-6 (paperback)
Subjects: Real estate investment – Australia
          Real property – Australia
          Wealth
Dewey Number: 332.6324

All rights reserved. Except as permitted under the Australian Copyright Act 1968 (for example, a fair dealing for the purposes of study, research, criticism or review), no part of this book may be reproduced, stored in a retrieval system, communicated or transmitted in any form or by any means without prior written permission. All inquiries should be made to the publisher.

Internal design by Production Works
Printed in Australia by McPherson's Printing
10 9 8 7 6 5 4 3 2 1

DISCLAIMER: The material in this publication is of the nature of general comment only, and does not represent professional advice. It is not intended to provide specific guidance for particular circumstances and it should not be relied on as the basis for any decision to take action or not take action on any matter which it covers. Readers should obtain professional advice where appropriate, before making any such decision. To maximum extent permitted by law, the author and publisher disclaim all responsibility and liability to any person, arising directly or indirectly from any person taking or not taking action based upon the information in this publication.

ABOUT THE AUTHOR

Philippe Brach, founder and CEO of Multifocus Properties & Finance, is a successful property investor who turned his passion for property into a unique investor-focused business. His 25-year background in corporate finance and accounting, as well as his experience as a property investor, real estate agent and finance broker, gives him the perfect profile to help investors in all aspects of property ownership. In particular, he can ensure that investment strategy, financial set-up, ownership structure and sourcing performing properties form a seamless plan that optimises potential for growth and preserves benefits associated with managing a portfolio.

www.multifocus.com.au

ACKNOWLEDGMENTS

I would like to express my gratitude to the many people who saw me through this book; to all those who provided support, talked things over, read, wrote, offered comments and assisted in the editing, proofreading and design.

In particular, I would like to thank my wife Claire for her unwavering support and assistance during the writing of this book. Without her constant sound advice and content review, this book would have been written in half the time!

Contents

Chapter 1: You will never work a day in your life... 1

STAGE 1: PLANNING – Getting ready to invest 15
Chapter 2: Money – It all starts here 21
Chapter 3: How finance can make or break your success 40
Chapter 4: Empowerment through education 54
Chapter 5: Defining your investment strategy 67

STAGE 2: ACCUMULATION – Finding proven property performers 81
Chapter 6: Designing your ultimate portfolio 85
Chapter 7: Choosing the right property 97

STAGE 3: TRANSITION – Minimising your risk and maximising your profits 111
Chapter 8: The most costly property investing risks and how to mitigate them 117
Chapter 9: Is there a *wrong* way to invest? 132

STAGE 4: DRAWDOWN – Creating your ultimate wealth 147
Chapter 10: Transition to wealth and retirement 151
Chapter 11: Educate and consolidate 163
Chapter 12: Where to from here? 175

Index 183

CHAPTER 1

You will never work a day in your life…

ARE YOU FAMILIAR with the saying, 'If you love what you do, you'll never work a day in your life'? It's a bit of a cliché, I know – and granted, no one has a job or a career that they love 100 per cent of the time. But, I believe I'm one of the lucky ones, because I can say that this phrase rings very true for me.

My career started more than 35 years ago, when I began working for an international hotel group in my home country of France. My role with that company took me around the world, from Paris, to London, Bangkok, Sydney, Tokyo and back to Sydney, where I finally settled in my own little piece of paradise.

I began working with this hotel group in the corporate finance department. After more than two decades of learning the ins and outs of the finance industry on an international scale, I can confidently call myself an expert on the subject!

Fortunately, I also happened to really enjoy it. My love affair with finance (if you could call it that) really took off when I was sent to London for six years to help grow the group's small presence in the UK. It was the beginning of a career where I was always in 'pioneering' positions, helping to set up accounts and finance in new offices around the world.

Talking about love affairs, it was also at that time that I met Claire, whom I first recruited as an accountant for our company and then eventually married. Everything was going perfectly well in my life.

When the company saw Asia as a big development area for the future, I was tapped to move to Bangkok to help establish the finance department, once again creating systems to manage the accounting, finance, purchase and acquisitions processes. The great thing about starting in a new country is that you are pretty much left to your own devices and, although I did not realise it straight away, it was the best environment for me. It allowed me to work the way I liked and be happy at work. I was there for three years with my wife Claire who also enjoyed the expat life to the full.

My next role saw us land in Sydney for several years before we moved to Japan for another few years. These were wonderful times and I count myself as exceptionally lucky to have had that time travelling the world while I built my career. But, after all those years of working long and hard while also exploring new places, Claire and I decided that it was time to settle down and call somewhere 'home'.

When I told my boss how I was feeling, I didn't know what to expect – but he gave me an incredible opportunity. The company had a presence in cities all around the world, so he simply said, 'Tell us where you want to settle down and we'll make it happen for you.'

The move that changed our lives – forever

How many people get this kind of opportunity?! So I took a moment to consider my options. I remember sitting with my wife in our residence in Tokyo, having a glass of wine, as we discussed where we wanted to go next. We had already lived in so many amazing, cosmopolitan cities; where would our next move take us? You can picture us looking at a globe and pointing at locations. But to be honest, it only took us about five minutes to make our decision. We knew that Australia was where we wanted to be.

The next thing we knew, my company was arranging my transfer to Sydney. After this, I spent another 10 years working for the group, based in the Harbour City. I spent my days working in mergers and acquisitions, travelling frequently to and from Asia, assessing deals and doing due diligence for the ever-expanding hotel group.

From a personal perspective, during this time we also set down some roots. When we knew we were going to make Sydney 'home', we decided to anchor ourselves to the city in the best possible way, adopting three dogs, all beagles – and getting a mortgage!

Working as an expat senior executive for so many years, I had a great borrowing capacity and a fair amount of savings in the bank. Once we were settled, I started to look at what we could do with our money to make it work for us as hard as possible.

Things I learned about negative gearing

That's when I learnt about the notion of negative gearing, which is unique to Australia. There is a similar system in Canada, but no one does it quite like the Aussies; the way that negative gearing is set up here is unique. I had never come across negative gearing before I moved to Australia, and that's saying something, because

I spent so much time working in all things finance, money and numbers in many international markets.

I thought that the whole concept of negative gearing was very clever. It was a win–win situation for everyone. The tax office gives you a yearly tax break to entice you to invest in property, and at the end of your investment journey the government collects capital gains tax (CGT) (when you sell your properties) and therefore the government claws their loss back – and more!

Obviously, as property values will have increased, you still make a handsome profit and the government gets back what it gave you over time. So, contrary to popular belief, negative gearing was not designed as a tax reduction scheme (some people even mistakenly call it tax avoidance) but as a tax deferment scheme.

CoreLogic published a report in 2016, called the 'Profile of the Australian Residential Property Investor', showing that the federal government did forgo about $3.5 billion in taxes through negative gearing, but they collected capital gains taxes on over $50 billion worth of gains! Even if we assume an effective tax rate of 10 per cent (which is very low), this represents a CGT collection of $5 billion at the minimum. Not a bad deal!

This does not include the state and territory governments' income in stamp duty and land taxes. This same report also highlights how little rental housing state and federal governments have to provide because of this arrangement.

Also, don't forget that tax concessions actually allow rents to be lower than if they did not exist. So renters also benefit. The whole thing is a great concept.

Although property is the most heavily taxed asset class in Australia, investing in real estate can actually be very attractive for everyone concerned.

To me, this was just the beginning of my new way forward.

Slow and steady wins the race? Not quite

Once I understood how negative gearing worked, I was hooked. I started building upon my education and before long, I was going on a shopping spree; I actually bought seven properties in six months! Later on, I discuss the fact that I should have done a little more research – or better yet, I should have found a very educated mentor to guide my decisions, rather than getting a little bit of advice from everyone I turned to before just diving right in.

I got my start in real estate investing by leveraging equity in my own home. My whole property investing strategy was based around the fact that I wanted to use what I had – my equity – to create a passive income stream that would one day replace my active income. In other words, I wanted to create an income that would continue without me having to go to work.

With seven properties in my portfolio in a matter of months, I think you could safely say I was addicted to real estate. Looking back, I think I was a little 'aggressive' in my acquisition strategy, but I had – and still have – an unflinching trust in the numbers.

What the numbers showed me was that, although there are risks in any investments, real estate risks were quite acceptable to me, and the likelihood of making a big mess of it was fairly low. This is because, unlike shares, you are not at risk of losing everything if the market turns south. Property values might decrease but they don't collapse in a matter of days. Also, tax concessions cushion any bad news. We will cover this later in the book.

I was becoming one of 'those guys' – you know, the people you speak to at barbecues on the weekends, who can't stop talking about whatever it is they're passionate about? That's when I had a huge realisation. Many of the friends I was chatting to at barbeques and social dinners were smart people, but they didn't invest in property – because they simply didn't understand it well enough.

Property is a much more involved asset class than shares, for instance, because you are investing in expensive assets that you cannot move quickly. Property is said to be an 'illiquid' asset. Shares are lower in cost and you can buy and sell them online at the click of a mouse. Property transactions take weeks or months to settle. This means you need to plan further ahead, and you need to know a lot more and be better prepared.

Helping others to invest

Many people don't have the time (or the interest) to learn everything you need to learn to prosper in property, so I started helping my friends navigate the world of real estate.

I started educating people. What really got me excited was when I explained to someone how it all works. I would start at the beginning with the basics, then go on to discuss how much they needed to get into property, what their cash flow would be like and how they would ultimately make money from their investments.

And they would 'get it'.

You can see when someone clicks. It's almost like a light bulb switching on above their head. Their eyes light up and suddenly you are all on the same page. It is such a great feeling (both for me and for the person I'm working with) to reach this point!

As much as I was addicted to property and the results I was achieving there, I also became addicted to educating people about real estate as well. I was a landlord seven times over and I was ready for a career change, and so that is when I decided to work for myself and launch Multifocus Properties & Finance.

The business was launched in 2005 with a handful of friends and colleagues as my first clients. I expected a slow start as I got the business off the ground, but things took off quite quickly. There was, and still is, a strong demand for learning how to prosper from property using simple, straightforward strategies.

Now more than ever, I find myself living out that phrase quoted earlier: 'If you love what you do, you'll never work a day in your life,' and this could not be truer for me. I'm very passionate about finance, money and real estate, because I know what is possible when you open yourself up to the idea of creating wealth through these means. The wealth, the choices, the lifestyle and the freedoms you can create in your life, once you learn how to properly master your finances, are extraordinary. I have learnt through personal experience that with the right education, strategy and action, absolutely anything you dream of is possible with property.

That is why I have written this book: to share with you what I have learned, and to break down and explain the process of building your portfolio and generating wealth through property.

Why should you listen to me?

If there is one thing we know about property investing, it is the fact that it is a very, very cluttered marketplace.

When I was starting out as an investor in the early 'noughties', it was quite a different landscape. There was a handful of property 'mentors' and buyer's agents in the market, but it was nothing like it is today.

Now, there are dozens (if not hundreds) of property 'experts' touting their strategies for success. It seems like everyone has a different method too, with complicated formulas, strategies and guidelines to follow. The result is that it can be hard to know who to trust.

This is one of the reasons why, when I meet with a new client, we go through their situation and I outline a process for them to get from where they are now to where they want to be in the future. If they then decide to work with me, great. If they decide to take the roadmap we have created and make their own way in property, then that's fine too. I am a firm believer in 'giver's gain'. I love helping people to make huge strides towards their financial goals, and by joining forces with my team, I believe you will fast track your results. But I also understand that everyone is at a different point in their journey and going it alone suits some better than others.

In addition to my real estate qualifications, I have a diploma in finance broking and I obtained my own Australian Credit Licence under the Australian Securities and Investments Commission (ASIC). The main reason I did this was because I found that it is quite hard to recommend a property to someone – even a very high-quality, well-performing property – if you know nothing about the person sitting in front of you. I needed to change the way we approached investing in real estate.

Tailoring an individualised approach

The way I approach investment is to start by asking: 'What is your situation now, and what would you like it to be?' From there, I can help an investor find the right property investments to help them reach their financial goals.

Think about it this way; if a person has a borrowing capacity of $350,000, there is no point in recommending that they buy a two-bedroom apartment in inner city Sydney, is there? Because no such property exists in this location at this price!

To genuinely help someone make a smart and strategic investment, you need to know where they are at financially in regards to obtaining a loan from a lender. Then you can help them reach their goals in the safest possible way, without overstretching their finances.

I did my training to become a real estate agent and a finance broker before I even hired a single staff member. It was the perfect foundation for launching Multifocus Properties & Finance as it meant I had everything I needed to run my business successfully: a broad understanding of numbers and taxation, a background in finance and accounting, and the qualifications required to guide people forward with their property investments.

What is more, I understand property investing from a personal perspective, because I am an investor myself. I feel as if I have the complete set of skills I need to actually be able to help others to invest. Since launching Multifocus Properties & Finance, I am pleased to say I have been able to help countless people take their next steps towards financial freedom.

Since making that leap-of-faith decision to strike out on my own and leave the comfort of my corporate career, I can honestly say that I have no regrets.

I have never sold any of my properties from within my portfolio, so everything I have bought over the years, I still own today. If I could go back and do things differently, perhaps I would not have bought every single asset I bought. Maybe I would have jumped on other opportunities instead. I don't know.

None of that really matters now – you cannot change the past. What I do know for certain is that every purchase I have settled on and every decision I have made has led me to where I am today.

This is what property can do for you…

To me, one of the biggest successes any investor can have is the ability to genuinely understand where they are going. My deep understanding of property investing allows me to structure my investments in the best possible way, so that they purposefully move me closer towards my goals.

I will give you an example. As it stands right now, I have got more than a dozen properties in my portfolio, and most of these properties are managed from one bank account, which is a line of credit. To that line of credit account, every rental payment goes in and every expense comes out – for each and every property.

This makes my investments very easy to manage, because it allows me to segregate all my investment cash flow from my private finances.

It may seem like a small part of the overall process, but this is a significant benefit when managing a large property portfolio. The way my investments are set up, I could actually add another dozen properties to the mix and it wouldn't change the way I manage my affairs!

This has made property investing a very calm and stress-free experience for me. The process of creating wealth and generating profits through real estate is rarely stressful, and I think this is largely due to the fact that I have structured the management of my portfolio so well. Of course, you always have teething problems when doing any business transactions, but once a property is up and running, it just ticks over.

I teach all of my clients to do the same. It is yet another reason why I love having my finance broking licence, as it gives me the opportunity to understand my clients' needs and create holistic solutions that work for them now and well into the future.

In the pages of this book, I want to show you how, using a simple step-by-step process, you can invest in property smartly and successfully. There are no gimmicks, no crazy strategies, no high-risk 'schemes', just straightforward advice and guidance to help you get from A to B.

For instance, I want to share with you one of my investments. I would say this is one of my biggest success stories, as it shows how you can boost your profits by thinking outside the box.

A positive example

When I was just starting out as an investor, I knew I had a good borrowing capacity and I wanted to experiment. As I mentioned earlier, I bought a number of properties in a six-month period. At the time, I knew I wanted to buy different assets so I bought a little of everything; a house-and-land package, an existing property, a new apartment, a retirement unit, the list goes on.

One of the properties I bought was a townhouse that was located close to a major university in Brisbane – the University of Queensland, located at St Lucia, a few kilometres from the CBD. I could see that the student market was strong in this area, and would help to deliver a steady stream of tenants my way. The fact that students have a reputation for being reckless did not bother me, and I (or I should say my local real estate managing agent) have never had any trouble with any of them.

That said, I did not want to buy a specific student accommodation investment property, because these types of investments are very restrictive. Typically, banks do not like them and so will ask for much higher deposits. They are also notoriously difficult to sell, as they only suit one set of buyers: cashed up investors. Worse still, there is very little capital growth in these types of assets. With all of this information at hand, I knew that a student property was not for me – but a property that appealed to students was!

I paid $370,000 for my three-bedroom townhouse in 2004. At that time, it was already tenanted with a local coffee shop owner who was paying $380 per week. The tenant was regularly defaulting on his rental payments, so I got the property manager to evict him pretty quickly. I decided to target students as my next tenants, which meant furnishing the home with basic furniture such as sofas and beds.

I immediately rented out the property to students – and my rent skyrocketed. It went from $380 per week to $530. By 2016 I was getting $650 a week for the property, which made it well and truly positively geared. This is a great example of how strong, local market knowledge and a clear investment strategy can deliver fantastic, highly profitable results. The property itself has substantially grown in value because of its location, so it ticks all the boxes.

A negative example

Now that I have shown you the positive results that can be achieved, I also want to show you what not to do.

This example relates to another of my early investments. One of the first properties I bought, back when I went on a huge buying spree, was a retirement unit for over-55s.

It was on the market for around $100,000, which seemed like an absolute steal. I ended up paying $97,000 for the property – this was back in 2004 – and it rented well from the beginning at $200 a week.

Here is what I did not factor in, though. When you buy a 'non traditional' property like this, it means you are buying something a little different to normal. As soon as you deviate from the mainstream residential property, banks become restrictive. I ended up paying more interest on the loan I took out on the property and I had to borrow less than I wanted (only 70 per cent of the purchase price). However, the rental yield (at 10.7 per cent) was just overriding these considerations.

This type of accommodation is designed for retirees who do not have many assets. They have not been able to retire in their own home, so they are renting their accommodation in a complex with like individuals (other retirees), which suits their lifestyle. The complex provides private accommodation, obviously, but it also provides many other amenities, such as laundry services, meals and activities. As a result, there are many common areas such as dining rooms, meeting halls and community laundries. These areas cost quite a lot to maintain, so the body corporate fees are substantially higher than they are in a standard residential complex.

Therein lies the financial catch. I only paid $97,000 for the property and today the rental return is strong at $260 per week – but the body corporate fees are very high. It still provides a positive cash flow and it is not a terrible investment, but if given the chance to go back, I probably would not buy into this type of investment again. It has not as yet yielded much by way of capital growth, so although it does not cost me anything to run, it does not help me get ahead in life.

This is what I was referring to earlier: by rushing in I didn't fully investigate what I was buying.

These types of missteps happen in property and with the right strategies in place, you can overcome almost anything; in my experience, property is a fairly forgiving asset.

It is my hope that after reading this book, you will have a crystal-clear idea of what you would like to achieve as a property investor and a strong idea of the strategies you would like to use to get ahead. At the very least, you should walk away with some inspiration of what is possible, after learning about the incredible profits you can achieve as a smart property investor.

STAGE 1: PLANNING

Getting ready to invest

THE FIRST STAGE in your property journey as an investor is the planning phase.

Planning your property portfolio may not sound like an exciting topic but believe me, it is a crucial part of the process. When you start to understand how investing works and how you can grow your wealth through strategic preparation at this early stage of the game, planning suddenly becomes a whole lot more interesting!

Ideally, you will want to consult a financial planner to help you work out exactly where your superannuation is headed, what your other investment income will be, and what reasonable value of investments you should work towards accumulating to achieve the retirement income you want.

Along with these considerations, the following pages will help you work through the process of planning your property investment strategy.

This essential first step towards creating property wealth is often overlooked, which is very dangerous, because planning sets the foundation for your entire property trajectory.

It amazes me that people will spend hundreds of thousands of dollars, quite possibly spending the most money they will ever spend in one transaction in their lifetime, without carefully thinking about what they are hoping to achieve.

You cannot just buy real estate in the hope that it will go up in value; property investing does not work like that. Instead, you need to discover what investing in property is about: how it works, how negative gearing works, how to leverage your finances and how to understand all of the factors that contribute to property growth.

Once you have this broad understanding, you can put together your strategy based on your numbers and your plan. You then move into the accumulation phase, which is when you actually buy properties. As I said, many people start out by buying properties and then they think about what their plans are for their investments later; let me tell you, this is not the ideal way to go!

Part of the planning phase is to figure out what your end goal is going to be. For most people this involves answering the question: 'How much passive income do I want to achieve from my portfolio's rental income when I retire?'

For the sake of simplicity throughout this book, we are going to assume an end goal of $2 million worth of property. Your goal may be different to this, and with the steps and processes outlined in the following chapters, you will be able to get an idea of a figure that works for you.

We are using the figure of $2 million because for the majority of Australians, this will allow for a comfortable retirement. We are ignoring inflation and present/future values to keep the calculations easy to follow; needless to say, a figure of $2 million in today's money could be worth twice that amount in a few decades' time.

As an investor you always want to work backwards. This means calculating how many properties you need (and what their cumulative value needs to be), in order to deliver your ideal outcome (an income of $X) in your pocket when you retire.

The safest way to look at it is to assume that you have got money in the bank and the long-term term deposit rate is around 5 per cent. Rental yields on most property investments tend to hover between 4 per cent and 6 per cent, so 5 per cent is a good average for simple calculations.

With $1 million in cash in the bank and a 5 per cent return, you would receive $50,000 per year in passive income (i.e. interest).

With $2 million in cash in the bank and a 5 per cent return, you would receive $100,000 per year in passive income.

With no mortgage in retirement, $100,000 (in today's money) would make for a great standard of living, wouldn't you agree? Later in this book we will look at converting this into a number of properties.

So let's get into the planning phase. Think of this like planning a holiday: you are deciding where to go, what to see and how to experience as much as possible. But instead of ending up with the memories from a two-week vacation, you are setting up your entire financial future – with many future holidays to be enjoyed!

CHAPTER 2
Money – It all starts here

IT MAY SURPRISE you to know that when you are investing in property, the actual piece of real estate you buy is the absolute last piece of the puzzle.

When I am meeting with a new client, during a 90-minute long property investing strategy session, we spend only the last few minutes talking about the actual location and type of property they should buy.

Why? Because the truth about investing in real estate is that it is never really about property: it is about finance. This is true of just about every asset you desire in life. For instance, if you do not have a savings account with a balance that ends in multiple zeroes, or a good job, you cannot just walk into a car dealer to buy a brand-new Mercedes without finance, can you?

Finance is what drives everything when creating wealth, and without access to finance you cannot go anywhere. So what personal financial factors can impact your investment journey?

In general terms, when you go to the bank to get a loan to fund your investments, you need to pretty much play along with their rules – and there are plenty of them.

Three key lending criteria

When a bank is looking at someone's application, they are looking at three things: *security*, *capacity* and *capital*.

You'll notice that only one of these points, the first one, actually relates to the property. The quality of the *security* is undoubtedly important. If you are looking at buying a million-dollar property located 300 kilometres west of Cobar, the banks are going to be nervous. They have a duty to minimise their risk and an expensive house located in a remote town is going to be much harder to sell than an apartment in the middle of Sydney's CBD, therefore it is considered to be a higher risk.

Remember: banks are assessing your application at the very outset from a 'worst case scenario' perspective. They have to consider their ability to sell the home, easily and efficiently, if they are forced into a position of having to repossess the asset.

For this reason, investing in a good quality property in a popular, sought-after location is important. But more about this later!

The next factor is your *capacity* – or more precisely your borrowing capacity, which essentially is your ability to repay your loan.

Banks are really simple beasts; they love consistency and stability. They love nothing more than an applicant who can show them a long history of receiving a regular income.

Lenders are impressed by consistency and stability of income. The bank will review your situation and paint a 'worst case scenario' picture in which you go out and spend all your money in one day. If that were to happen and you have no regular income coming in, then they have no assurance that you will be able to repay your debt.

Without enough income to support your application, your ability to service your loan is substantially diminished – and as a result, so is your borrowing power. And that means your property finance application is left dead in the water.

The third consideration is your capacity to access *capital* and put down a deposit. They want to see that you are responsible with money and that you are an astute saver. Capital can be in the form of savings or equity in a property.

Now, this part is really important: all three of these factors have to be looked at independently from each other. Having two out of three factors working on your side often will not be enough to get your application approved.

Let's say you have great borrowing capacity, a significant amount of savings and a plan to buy an expensive property located 300 kilometres west of Cobar. You may not get that loan.

Similarly, you could have a property that is situated in central Sydney with a waiting list of dozens of potential tenants, plus you have plenty of borrowing capacity… But if you do not have a decent deposit, you won't get a loan.

And if you have a great property and a hefty deposit, but you do not have a strong income position to support your ability to repay your debts, then you won't get a loan from the bank.

These three factors must work in collaboration with each other, and when they don't, it can be very frustrating for the borrower. You can now guess that one of these factors is going to be your weak point. When building a portfolio of properties, which are you going to start running out of first – your borrowing capacity or your deposit money? Once you know, you can start working on how to strengthen the weak link.

I recall a client in the past who said, 'It is true I have little income, but I have plenty of equity in my property and I have half a million dollars in cash in the bank – why won't the bank lend me any money?'

This is because he confused capacity and capital. You need both to be successful, and you need both for the banks to lend you money!

They keep changing the rules

To make matters even more confusing, banks and lenders change the rules of engagement frequently – and I mean, all the time.

For example, in 2015, at the behest of the Australian Prudential Regulation Authority (APRA), the banks across Australia began implementing stricter guidelines when lending to investors.

I worked with one of my clients to gain him a pre-approval for a loan for the amount of $2 million with the Commonwealth Bank (CBA). Unfortunately, he was not quite ready to buy and so he let that pre-approval expire – which turned out to be very bad timing.

By the time he came back to us with the property he wanted to buy, the lending criteria from CBA had changed to such a point that he was only approved to borrow $850,000. He lost more than half of his borrowing power in a matter of months, purely due to external factors.

I have said it before and I will say it again: investing successfully is rarely about the real estate you buy, it is driven by the finance that funds your goals. So what can you do to put your best financial foot forward when applying for a mortgage?

Preparing to invest in property in five easy steps

Every investor is going to be in a different starting position, but I would like to give you a broad understanding of the five key criteria that banks look at when deciding whether or not to give you a loan.

1. Your income and debt

Strategy: Maximise your income and minimise your debts

This comes back to my earlier point: you need to have the capacity to repay your loans in order for banks to feel confident lending to you.

I refer to my earlier example of the client who has half a million dollars in the bank. Because he has a small, regular income his borrowing capacity is only $200,000. His capacity to borrow from the bank is significantly reduced due to the fact that he has a weak income, despite having a large deposit.

If you are in this situation, how do improve your position to borrow more money? There are two options available to you.

First, you need to get more income – it is genuinely the best way to boost your application. Either you work more hours, get a promotion, change jobs, or consider investing with a partner or a member of your family to improve the income situation on the loan application. Anything that will bring more income to the table for the bank is the only way you are going to get a better loan.

Do not forget that a bank will take into account some – usually 80 per cent – of the rental income from the investment property you are about to buy.

The other thing you can do to improve the bank's view of your situation is to reduce your expenses. When you go to a lender, they are going to look at how much you earn and also how much you spend. Reducing your outgoings, including your regular bills and your debts, means you have fewer financial obligations and, therefore, the capacity to take on a bigger loan.

To calculate your cost of living, banks look at your declared expenses on your loan application and compare these to the Household Expenditure Measure (HEM). They will take into account whichever is the highest. As a rough guide, for a single person the minimum HEM is around $1,200 per month; for a couple with one child, the minimum is about $3,000 per month. For some investors, you may need to be frugal with your living expenses and make sure that your cost of living is as close to the minimum as possible.

How your credit card kills your borrowing power

For every credit card you have, the bank assumes that you repay 3 per cent of the limit of the credit card per month. They do not care about the balance of your credit card, they care about the limit, because as far as they are concerned a $40,000 limit is a $40,000 debt.

If you have got a $40,000 credit card limit, the bank assumes a repayment of $1,200 a month. That is $1,200 shaved off your capacity to repay your loan, which can dramatically impact your borrowing capacity.

For this reason, I always advise my clients who are looking for more borrowing capacity to reduce their credit card liability to the minimum amount they are comfortable with. If you have a $40,000 credit card limit with a debt of $1,800, you could reduce the limit to $2,000 and instantly increase your borrowing power by about $180,000!

By the way, the same rule applies for other personal debts such as a car loan, a personal loan or a store credit card. Minimising or eliminating these debts is one of the easiest and most effective ways to improve your loan application with your bank.

For example, if you have some equity in your home and you have also contracted a personal loan, it makes good sense to consolidate your personal debt into your home loan. Monthly repayments are much lower on a 30-year home loan at 4 to 5 per cent than a personal loan over 7 years at 13 per cent, and as a result your borrowing capacity increases.

Did you know?

A credit card debt of just $5,000 can have the impact of reducing your mortgage borrowing power by up to $25,000. Add up the total limit of all of your credit cards and refer to Table 2.1 below to see what impact those debts could be having on your mortgage application. How much more could you borrow if you got your credit cards and personal debts under control?

Table 2.1: Impact of credit card debt on borrowing capacity

Credit card limit	Reduction to borrowing power
$1,000	$5,000
$2,000	$10,000
$3,000	$15,000
$5,000	$25,000
$10,000	$50,000
$20,000	$100,000
$30,000	$150,000
$40,000	$200,000
$50,000	$250,000
$100,000	$500,000

2. Your savings

Strategy: Create a savings goal to build a property deposit

When I begin working with a new client, one of the first questions they generally ask is, 'How much deposit do I really need to buy an investment property?'

Typically, the answer will depend on how much you plan to borrow from the bank. First, you need to decide what LVR (loan to value ratio) you plan to borrow to. If you borrow 80 per cent or less from the bank, you won't be required to pay Lenders Mortgage Insurance (LMI). If you borrow more than 80 per cent, you will be required to pay this premium, which actually protects the bank (not you) if you default on your loan.

As a guideline, to buy a $500,000 property, if you borrow 80 per cent from the bank, you will need about $130,000 to cover your $100,000 deposit and associated buying costs (see Table 2.2 below), such as stamp duty.

Table 2.2: Property buying costs to budget for

Stamp duty (varies state by state)	Ranges from $17,000 in Queensland to $26,000 in Victoria on a $500,000 property, for Australian residents
Lenders mortgage insurance (loans over 80 per cent)	Between 1 to 5 per cent of the loan amount
Legal and conveyancing fees	Around $2,000 to purchase
Finance and loan application fees	Up to $1,000
Building, defects and pest inspection fees	$500 to $600
Depreciation schedule	$350 to $800

This is obviously a huge amount of money. You do not need to have access to the whole amount in cash – many people leverage equity from their own home or an existing investment property to use as a property deposit. Even so, this figure can be very discouraging as a financial goal!

If saving $130,000 seems too unrealistic, you have a couple of options. You can lower your buying expectations and aim to invest in a more affordable property at around $300,000 (if you can find a good one at that price!); this would reduce your deposit and buying costs to between $75,000 and $80,000.

Or you could borrow up to 90 per cent from the bank, which is quite a common strategy for investors. With this approach, you would need a deposit of around $80,000 for a property valued at $500,000, or $45,000 for a $300,000 property. You will also need to pay lender's mortgage insurance (LMI), which is a one-off fee payable on loans over 80 per cent as a risk protection measure for your bank.

If you want to borrow more than 80 per cent, lenders start getting nervous and their policy is to reinsure themselves with one of the reinsurance companies. Some banks also reinsure loan risk internally, meaning you will pay an internal risk fee rather than an external insurance fee.

Banks will also want to see some 'genuine savings', to confirm that you are a good saver. They will ask to check your last three months' savings statements. The balance of your savings should be at least 5 per cent of the purchase price of the property. Equity in a property counts as genuine saving.

Note that if you do intend to borrow more than 80 per cent, LMI is an insurance premium that is paid by the borrower, but that protects the bank. Many people misunderstand that when they pay an LMI premium their loan is secured, but it provides them no coverage whatsoever. Instead, it gives the bank a guarantee that they will not lose money if you stop paying your mortgage.

Did you know?
If you are renting and you want to buy an investment property, some lenders will accept the fact that you are regularly paying your rent as part of your genuine savings test. Speak to your broker to see if this strategy may help you!

Also, most lenders will allow you to 'capitalise' the LMI fee, which means they will add it to your loan – so it does not have to come out of your savings. The limit is usually 90 per cent inclusive of LMI, but some lenders will offer 90 per cent plus capitalised LMI.

3. Your job status

Strategy: Learn to play the 'consistency' game with lenders

Here is the reality of the situation: it is a lot easier to get a mortgage if you are employed in a stable salaried position than if you are self-employed.

It all comes down to risk. For someone on a payroll, gaining finance approval is quite straightforward. It generally does not matter what kind of profession you are working in, as banks do not discriminate against that. What they are looking for is consistency of earnings, as the bank wants to know that you are capable of repaying the loan on a long-term basis.

If you are self-employed, banks are less confident about your long-term income potential, so most of them will want to see two years' worth of tax returns that show a good, consistent income. Within those two years, if there is a difference in profit of more than 20 per cent, they will take the lowest of the two years as your income.

This 20 per cent policy is really important because it can make a huge difference to your application. For instance, I recall meeting with a client who said, 'I earn $77,000 working for myself as a car mechanic.' When he showed me his last two years' tax returns, they painted a different story.

The most recent financial year showed a $77,000 profit, but the year before showed only $50,000. As that is a difference of greater than 20 per cent between the two years' profit, the bank would only review his application with an income of $50,000. If the difference had been less than 20 per cent, they would have just averaged the two years' profit.

As you can imagine, being self-employed can be a real stumbling block towards getting finance approval. In fact, if you have recently started a business, for the first two years you may find it very difficult to get a home loan. For many self-employed people it could be challenging for an even longer period, because it will take a few years for your business to start earning a decent profit – and until you can show substantial profitability, you will not get a bank loan.

Why are the banks so hard on the self-employed? It is simply a form of self-protection. In their view, if you are self-employed, you are putting everything on the line, including your savings and your emergency buffers. If you take a sick day, you will not get paid any money. This makes them nervous.

Traditionally, banks have always been much harsher on self-employed people compared to people on a payroll, but it will be interesting to see how this evolves as the economy evolves. We now have more self-made millionaires and innovative entrepreneurs pushing new boundaries than ever, and the average life cycle for a salaried position is around two years.

Until the banks change their policies to keep up with changing times, however, the self-employed will need to come up with strategies to play the finance game. This means doing everything you can to present your application in the most positive light to banks and lenders.

It can also be difficult to get a loan if you are employed in a casual position, due to the bank's view that your income is inconsistent or unstable. Casual employees need to show some consistency of income over a period of time, usually two years.

Many self employed and casual workers resort to applying for 'low doc loans' where scrutiny is reduced, but interest rates are more expensive and LVRs cannot exceed 80 per cent.

Did you know?

If your employment history is anything other than long-term salaried employment, it is definitely in your best interests to work with a qualified mortgage broker who has experience working with investors. They can guide you through the process and advise you on steps you can take to improve your application's chance of success.

4. Your career history

Strategy: Demonstrate your commitment to your industry

Gone are the days when the majority of people will clock in at work with the same employer year-in, year-out, for 25-plus years. Lenders recognise this; in the new world order, continuing your employment with the same organisation for five years or more is considered a decent stint.

So, banks and lenders do not necessarily need to see longevity with the same employer in your loan application. What they do want to see however is proof that you are a low-risk applicant, as they want to be assured of your ability to repay your home loan. This is where job stability comes into the picture as it demonstrates that you are a stable prospect.

If you cannot prove that you have stayed in the same job for years, then demonstrating stable employment within one industry is the next best thing. If you have worked in marketing for 10 or 12 years, it shows commitment and responsibility – even if over that time you have worked for three or four different employers.

On the other hand, if your resume has you jumping from a marketing role to a sales job, to a stint working in the ski fields in Canada before you returned to Australia to work in office admin, lenders might get the impression that you are flighty or restless.

That is not to say that you will not be able to get a loan; the bank will look at a number of factors and your employment history is just one of them. Some banks will even consider giving you a mortgage with as little as two months of employment under your belt, especially if they can see you are a professional person. Other banks will insist on having six months at least before they give you a loan.

The overriding principle is consistency of income. If you are planning to buy a home in the next six to twelve months, do not go making a sudden career change, and definitely do not think about throwing in your job to start your own business.

Did you know?

Banks view each employment industry under a different risk profile. Typically, professional industries such as accounting, legal and medical are perceived as less risky. Loan applications from borrowers employed in these industries may be evaluated on less restrictive criteria, and some fees and charges may even be waived. As an example, most major banks are offering to waive LMI on loans with an LVR of up to 90 per cent for doctors. Speak to your broker or contact our office to see if these benefits may apply to you and your situation.

5. Your credit file

Strategy: Protect your reputation as if your financial life depends on it

Credit files are very important. In fact, they can make all the difference between your loan being approved or rejected.

Every single Australian resident has a credit record, which is stored with one of the credit agencies. These agencies collect data on people and they provide it to banks, lenders and other suppliers (e.g. Telstra) who pay for access to that information.

In the past, the only information a lender could find out about you from your credit record would be the number of times you have applied for a loan and the instances in which you did not pay a bill. For example, the information was shown along the lines of: 'On May 23, 2013, Jane Smith applied for a loan with ANZ for $15,000.'

This is called 'negative' reporting because it just reports the negative news (credit defaults when you fail to pay a bill on time) and the number of credit applications.

By looking at your record, no one could actually find out if you got approved for that credit card or loan. Until 2014, that is, when the way that credit is reported changed to 'positive' reporting.

Now, lenders will put a lot more information on your record. If your loan is declined for any reason, they will put that on your credit file. If you are late in paying your credit card bill, you are now rated on your credit card repayments, month by month for two years!

If your loan has been approved, it will be reported. If you are in arrears on a bill for a few months, it will be reported.

Overall, it is a lot more detailed and lenders can get a much better idea of your risk profile, based on the additional information. Many banks will even 'credit score' you, which means they will use their own algorithm to crunch all of their known data about you to come up with a credit score.

This allows them to come up with a robust profile of you, based on data from your credit profile and your credit score. Obviously if your score is bad, you will not get the loan.

For instance, I had a client who was a high-ranking officer in the Navy who was declined for finance. It turned out that he had a $25,000 default on his credit file, relating to a car lease he had refused to pay. He was being a bit pig-headed as he said, 'I had a car accident and I cannot see why I should keep paying the lease if I can no longer use the car.'

Well, that was not the view of the leasing company, obviously, so they kept sending him his monthly bill – and he kept ignoring it. They logged a $25,000 default on his credit file. When we tried to get the loan for him, it was a major disaster; come to think of it, he is lucky they did not initiate bankruptcy proceedings!

That situation was fairly clear-cut, but sometimes I have seen baffling results. I have had applicants who were squeaky clean and have never paid a bill late in their lives, but they were still declined on the basis of their credit score. The infuriating thing about this is that we really do not know why they were declined; we are only told that the application failed on credit scoring. It is really a case of 'computer says no!'

It can simply be a situation where someone has moved without leaving a forwarding address, which leads to a phone or energy bill going unpaid.

Factors that can impact your credit score include:

- Applying for too many credit cards or loans

- Managing too many personal debts
- Having a high number of debts compared to your income
- Carrying a high level of personal debt on an average or low income
- Having a very low net worth.

The good news is that there are some banks out there that do not credit score. When we work with people who are declined for finance due to poor credit scoring, which admittedly does not happen very often, we will help them apply with a lender that does not credit score.

What does your credit file look like?

Have you ever seen your credit profile? Do not worry if you have answered 'no'. In my experience, most people do not know what their credit file looks like, or even know where to go to find it.

It is great information to have at hand, however, so I definitely suggest you request a copy of your credit profile. It is as simple as visiting www.mycreditfile.com.au. Then put in the requested personal details and within around two weeks, they will send you your credit report for free. If you want to see it instantly, you can fast track the results for a small fee.

You can also subscribe to VEDA Advantage; this is what I do. Every time someone queries my credit record, I get an email. I recently refinanced four loans and I received four alerts, so I knew the lender was processing my application. It is very affordable (currently less than $100 per year), and it is a worthwhile investment.

Credit policies change all the time. During the Global Financial Crisis (GFC) when everyone was panicking, the banks actually became really, really tight with their lending criteria. I recall ANZ being particularly tough – if you had a default even as low as $10, they would decline the loan as their policy was to automatically decline for ANY default. Usually, if an unpaid debt is under $200, then lenders will be flexible.

You may manage your money very well, and therefore believe you do not need to check in and review your credit file. But the reality is, it only takes one small default on your report to impact your ability to get finance for years.

> ***Did you know?***
> When a bank runs a credit check, it also checks to see if you are the director of a company. Even if you only have a small share in a company, the bank can mark you as self-employed and can ask to see the full accounts of the company, to ensure it is profitable. This is because, as a company director, you have influence over the management of the business. This can impact your credit score so, when applying for finance, be sure to disclose everything.

Are you in a position to begin investing?

If you are not in a position to invest in property today, what steps do you need to take to get ready to invest tomorrow?

This is a question I field quite a lot. People come to us and say, 'I want to get on the property bandwagon – what can I do?'

Once I look at their situation, I can often see that they do not have enough money for a deposit, or they do not have the servicing to support a loan for the property they want to invest in. At this point I ask: what can we do to get you into a position to get the loan?

For example, I recently had a young couple come in who had a strong income position and a borrowing capacity of about

$1 million. However, because they were only just starting out in life, they only had $20,000 in savings to use as a deposit.

Remember, you need about $80,000 as an average figure to get into property if you borrow 90 per cent, so they were a long way off from that.

I asked them:

- Is there any way you could get a gift or a loan from mum and dad?
- Are you prepared to create a savings plan – and stick to it?
- What are your career prospects like: are you in a position to ask for a raise, or look for a new higher paying job, to thereby fast-track your savings?

With this particular couple, we worked out that they could save an additional $60,000 in about 18 months. With a clear savings plan in place and perhaps a small loan/gift from mum and dad, they would be in a position to buy their first investment in as little as 12 months.

In my experience, I have found that as long as you are keen and willing, there is always a way to make things happen. Goal-setting is very important as you prepare for investing. When working with our clients, we look realistically at how much they can save and how long it will take them to save the amount they need.

If you do not have adequate borrowing capacity, for instance, and you are a waiter earning an average income, you could look at opportunities to work for a big hotel chain where you are likely to get a promotion.

If you secure a promotion to restaurant manager, then you may have the income to buy a property. It always comes down to looking at your situation now, and looking at what your situation could be, so you can create the ideal environment to deliver the best possible outcome.

It is not unusual for me to receive calls from clients saying, 'Philippe, two years ago, you told me I needed to save $60,000. I have done it now – can we invest in property?'

Those calls are always brilliant to receive! It is such an achievement, as it demonstrates that when you are dedicated and committed to becoming a genuine investor, you are setting yourself up to do well in life.

CHAPTER 3

How finance can make or break your success

WE HAVE BEEN through the nuts and bolts of finance, which are the most essential building blocks of the whole property investing experience. Next I want to discuss some of the myths or fallacies to do with property investing, as many people do not understand how the smallest of decisions can have the biggest of impacts on their personal situation.

For instance, an area that continues to fool people is the myth of customer loyalty. Have you made the mistake of believing that because you have been with your bank for the last 20 years and because it is *your* bank, it will be easier for you to get a loan?

I am here to tell you: that is rubbish. In the past, perhaps a long history with a bank could have held some sway in getting your loan application across the line. In fact, customer loyalty can even work against you. Let me explain.

In the modern mortgage market, the bank – any bank – will

need you to 'tick the boxes' set out in their loan criteria. If you do not have the income to service your loan, your application will be declined. Your application will only be approved on merit, not because you have been with the bank for 20 years.

Having said that, they will definitely check your 'account conduct' – i.e. have you been paying your bills on time? Have you gone over your overdraft limit? This can play a part in the overall picture, but they will not look at your application more favourably because of your loyalty.

On the contrary, a bank will often look upon a potential new client who they can steal from a competitor in a much better light, because they take existing clients for granted.

Banks only get excited about their existing customers if they are at risk of losing them. When you are trying to refinance a loan or if you ask for a discharge form, you can bet they will suddenly be all over you, offering you a lower rate and other savings to prevent you from leaving.

Customer loyalty is the first fallacy that people have about banks and finances, but it is certainly not the last. Below are a few other finance and money myths and misconceptions people often have, which I want to clear up.

Over-estimating your income

A big mistake that people make, especially when they are self-employed, is to over-estimate how much they earn.

For instance, I might have a borrower say to me, 'I earn $100,000 a year.' When they show me their accounts, however, it looks like their annual profit is as low as $30,000 or $40,000. When I question them, they will say, 'Well, $100,000 is how much I am going to make this financial year, I am doing really well.' It turns out that last year they made $70,000, which was reduced to $40,000 when they deducted all of their work-related expenses.

Here is the problem: banks do not look forward, they look back in time. They look at your track record when they are assessing your income, not at what you are going to earn this year. As we have already discussed in Chapter 2, they also like to see at least two years' worth of tax returns and if your income varies substantially between those two years, they will generally go with the lower number to mitigate their risk.

When I get clients who are self-employed, the first thing I ask them for is a copy of their tax return. Invariably, the number they have given me as their income is not correct – at least not from the bank's point of view – as they have often got an over-inflated opinion of their own performance. Unfortunately, the banks do not buy that.

Confusing bank advice with strategy advice

We have been lured into a false sense of security over time to believe that if we can walk into a bank branch and speak to people face to face, then we will get good service. People generally think that because they are speaking to the loan officer in the branch of a major bank, they are going to get someone very competent and knowledgeable advising them about their loan.

That is not always correct. The reality is, there is often a very high turnover of staff at the branch level. Bank staff get good training, there is no question about that, but a lot of them do not have experience behind them the same way that mortgage brokers do. Plus, they are only interested in one objective: getting you a loan. They do not generally have the experience, expertise or interest in advising you on how to structure your finances for the long term. All they can do, and have been briefed to do, is to give you a loan.

Assuming all lenders are the same

People think it does not matter which lender you go to; that they are all the same. They are not. I will get to this later on in this chapter when I discuss banks versus brokers, but for now I want to touch on the concept of all lenders being essentially the same.

In the same way that bank staff have varying levels of experience and expertise, banks and lenders differ in how they approach the market. Some lenders have a much lower-risk appetite than others.

As a very basic example of this, let's consider rental income. The rental income that you receive from your property may be $400 per week. Depending on your lender, they may accept your rental income as being:

- $320 per week – 80 per cent of actual rental income
- $300 per week – 75 per cent of real rental income
- $280 per week – 70 per cent, the maximum amount they will accept as rent for that suburb.

In terms of assessing your loan application, the difference between how each bank assesses rental income could have a huge impact on your loan approval. And yet, this is still one of the biggest and most common mistakes that comes up again and again.

It's not unusual to work out the borrowing capacity of a client according to the lending criteria of four to five banks and often come up with a wide range of numbers, starting from $300,000 with one lender up to $900,000 with another.

Pushing your borrowing capacity to the limit

Trying to push to get another loan when you are already at your limit is a common mistake I see people make.

Consider this. If you have a borrowing capacity of $1 million, do you think it is in your best interests to go out and borrow $1 million? Many people would answer 'yes'. Why not push the limits and maximise your lending during the accumulation stage, right?

Perhaps this works for some. However, let's say you are trying very hard to borrow as much as you can to buy as much as you can. In a low interest rate environment that is fine – but when interest rates start going up, people find themselves in strife.

Putting yourself under pressure by borrowing to your limit just to get an extra property is a mistake. I think investors should always leave some kind of reserve, either in cash or in borrowing capacity, to hedge their bets in the future.

I have heard people say, 'The bank does not want to lend me any money, what can I do? How can I get around it?' The bank may have a good reason for not lending them any money, the obvious one being that the borrower can't afford it! The bank wants your business so, if they say no, then there is usually a good reason for it.

I remember the good old days when we could borrow with what we called 'no doc loans'. All you had to do was give your name, address and the address of the property you were buying, and the bank would lend you 80 per cent of the value of the property. You did not have to justify your income – this was obviously before the GFC!

I know about these loans, because I used to have two loans that I obtained this way. The reason I had them was because I made exactly this mistake. I thought, 'The banks do not want to give me a loan, so I will go for a no doc loan where nobody is asking me any questions, and I will buy as many properties as I want.'

Luckily I only bought two. If I had hocked myself into sky-high debt, I could have been caught out and been massively overexposed. Fortunately, these days, no doc loans no longer exist, but they demonstrate the risks when people try to push too hard with financing.

Forgetting that rates will go up

In terms of pure risk, the biggest risk for all property owners is generally the same – the risk of interest rates rising.

When you get yourself into a market in a really low interest rate environment, everything can appear to be moving forward smoothly. But you can get caught out in a big way if you do not look at what your cash flow will be if interest rates go up by 1 per cent, 2 per cent or even more.

It is important to consider, before you get into any kind of financing, what would happen if rates went up by a significant amount. What would your cash flow be then? Can you still afford your mortgage repayments? Will your finances be stretched to the max trying to pay the bills or will you manage with plenty to spare?

At an interest rate of around 4 per cent, it is easy to find cash flow positive properties that will also deliver capital growth. As an example, for a $500,000 newish property with a yield of 5 per cent, an LVR of 90 per cent and an investor paying 39 per cent tax, the cash flow would be around $40 per week positive.

However, if interest rates were around 7 per cent, that same property becomes cash flow negative by about $100 per week. All of these calculations assume you are repaying the mortgage on an interest-only basis.

Now, an increase in rates may be something you can easily live with as an investor. But if you build your asset base and you have a portfolio of properties, you may then have four or five properties costing you $100 each per week. That is $500 that you have to find, each and every week.

It is not an issue if you have a plan that will allow you to absorb this amount easily. The most important thing for an investor is to execute an investment plan knowing exactly what the numbers are and how to adapt to an ever-changing environment.

These are the sorts of scenarios we map out with our clients before they invest, to ensure they do not end up with financial stress down the road.

Failing to understand risk management

The example I discussed above is a classic case of risk management. The risk is interest rate increase and the challenge is to come up with a strategy to manage this risk. One solution could be to fix your interest rate, or you could add a positively geared property to your portfolio to help pay for some of your property losses.

Whatever the solution is, you need to consider and plan for potential risks to eventuate as a property investor. It is not enough to say, 'Things are going well for me in this current environment'. You must also consider your ability to manage risk, and risk management means understanding your personal situation.

There are a lot of people out there marketing investment properties to inexperienced investors and, often when they are showing projections of potential returns from that property, they are only showing them at the current interest rate. We make sure that when we talk to our clients, we show them projections at today's rate and also show them what would happen if rates went up to 7 or 8 per cent. At least that way they know the numbers and they can base their strategy on how to deal with that situation if increases do eventuate. If they cannot manage that risk, then the investment they were considering does not make sense and they should not proceed and invest in that property.

These are just some of the misconceptions and beliefs that many people have surrounding property finance. There are many more, which we discuss in depth with our clients based on their individual situations.

Banks versus brokers: What you need to know

People often feel safe with their bank because it is a big machine. If they have a history with that lender, it can make a borrower feel more comfortable dealing with them for a mortgage – which is often a scary experience in itself (when else do you ever request hundreds of thousands of dollars from anyone?!).

Because banks have multiple big branches where you can walk in and 'experience' the brand, you can feel more safe and secure about partnering with them on big financial transactions. All of this creates a feeling of comfort and safety – but the truth is, it is a false sense of security.

Fact: when you go to a bank, they are trying to sell you their product (obviously!).

There are many, many loan products with different banks that might be more suitable for you, but your bank is going to try and sell you their product.

How can you decide if it is the right product for you? How can you tell whether their risk policy is suitable for you and your situation? How can you work out if your self-employed career means they are less likely to approve your loan, or whether the fact you have two properties already diminishes your borrowing power with this particular bank by 25 per cent?

There is no way to know all of this information – unless you use a mortgage broker.

The other option is to do all the work yourself. You can go to several banks and discuss your situation and see what your options are. Each one will give you a different outcome, I can almost guarantee it.

For example, I know an investor who owns a property in far north Queensland. She went to her own bank for a refinance and for a new loan, and they refused to proceed with her application based on serviceability: they felt she was too highly leveraged.

So she did some shopping around and found another lender, one with a different servicing calculator, and they agreed to lend her money. One of her properties was attached to a 70 per cent LVR and she was trying to increase it to 80 per cent, to withdraw the equity for another property purchase.

This bank proceeded with the application and everything appeared to be moving forward, until they realised the location of her existing property, that is. She wanted to refinance her rental home in far north Queensland and when the bank realised this, her application was halted. Why? Because this lender required a 50 per cent deposit for properties located in regional towns that they deemed risky, which included her town.

She has now had two finance applications knocked back (which is two marks on her credit report) and she is no closer to getting loan approval!

This is the risk you run when working with banks directly. When working with a qualified and experienced mortgage broker instead, they can negotiate all of these hurdles for you. Or better still, they will steer you in the direction of lenders who best suit your situation.

In the example above, a good finance broker would never have suggested to this investor that she apply for finance with a lender with risk-averse policies for far north Queensland.

Risk of cross-collateralising

Cross-collateralising always serves the lender but rarely serves the borrower. It involves cross-securitising your investment loan across two or more properties – usually your own home and your investment property.

For example, let's say you own your own home, which is worth $500,000 and has a mortgage of $300,000. You access $100,000 in equity to purchase an investment property.

Instead of refinancing your loan to 'extract' this equity and create a whole new financial structure for your investment property, you allow your bank to cross-collateralise your assets. The two properties are then stuck together.

When you buy your third property, you go to the same bank and do exactly the same thing, so you have now cross-collateralised three properties. As an investor you have three properties and three loans, all tied in knots.

This may not seem like a big risk – until you want to make a change. Imagine that you want to sell one property. The bank might say, 'Before you sell the property, I want to revalue your other two assets, to make sure whatever debts are left are still secured properly. If one of your properties has gone down in value, or the LVR of your portfolio changes, you might not be able to sell.'

Overall your portfolio has an LVR of 75 per cent, but selling that one property would leave your remaining property loans with an LVR of 83 per cent. The bank therefore refuses to allow you to sell – or will only let you divest the property on the condition that some of the proceeds go towards paying down your other loans.

In other words, they hold all the cards, because your loans are all tied up together.

It makes things very difficult if you want to sell a property, or refinance a loan, or make any changes to your property portfolio at all. This can become a huge risk and can create some very serious problems for property investors.

I had a client once who had seven properties cross collateralised with one of the 'big four' banks. He was a miner in Charters Towers, and I could not refinance him because it meant he would have to refinance seven properties at the same time.

The problem with this is that banks will always assess your loans at their own 'assessment rate'. The actual interest you are paying may be 5 per cent, but the bank will set their own, higher assessment rate (generally at least 2 per cent higher than the actual rate paid) to 'stress test' your mortgage and ensure you can still afford your loans if interest rates go up.

In this client's case, they added a 3 per cent premium to his actual interest rate and based on this assessment rate he was ineligible for new finance.

If the properties had not been cross-collateralised, I could have helped him restructure his finances piece by piece, refinancing with a better bank on this loan and another bank on that loan. Unfortunately, he was stuck.

Obviously, the banks like this situation because you then become a 'sticky' customer. You are sticky because it becomes harder and harder for you to go to another lender. In most cases, it is their default policy to cross-collateralise, which is actually quite naughty.

There may be big financial risks attached to structuring your finances in the wrong way, and it pays to get a good broker who understands how investment properties work. There are plenty of brokers in Australia, about 12,000 I believe, but only an experienced few are really good at structuring investment property loans.

Investment property loans can be a lot more complicated than the average home loan and they require a finance expert who understands how tax works and property investment works. So be sure to talk to an experienced professional who has been referred to you by happy clients.

How to find the right mortgage broker

In terms of mortgage brokers, as with every other service-provider, you have good mortgage brokers and you have below-average mortgage brokers. To find the right mortgage broker to work with, you should make sure you interview a potential broker properly because, depending on what you are trying to achieve (especially if you are trying to buy an investment property), a 'standard' broker will probably not be much help.

There is a lot more work involved when you are buying an investment property versus buying a home because you are talking about strategy. When you buy a home, you just get a loan, buy a home and off you go.

When you are buying an investment property you need to talk about structuring your loans so that you can maximise your money, develop future plans to redraw equity, learn how to use offset accounts to your advantage and understand how to repay your loans for maximum tax benefit, (using a tax strategy as advised by your accountant).

You also generally get higher levels of customer service when working with a mortgage broker. A banker might be able to chat with you about your needs at their branch but a broker can often come to you, at your workplace or home, or even visit you after hours or on weekends if needed.

Remember that there are different levels of brokers too. Some standard mortgage brokers are not experienced in working with investors and may not be able to give you the best advice either. What you need is a finance broker who specialises in investments; who knows the investment world and, ideally, who invests in property themselves. You will get a lot more value from this type of broker and have a much higher chance of gaining loan approval.

Just be careful whom you choose to work with. Make sure you interview them to ensure they have the following credentials:

- They have experience
- They own investment properties themselves
- They are industry qualified, i.e. a member of the Mortgage & Finance Association of Australia (MFAA) or the Finance Brokers Association of Australia (FBAA)
- They are up-to-date with the latest legislation and regulations.

A mortgage broker now has to have, as a minimum, a diploma in financial services, and therefore they are a lot better educated, which has put more confidence into the broking system. In 2010, around 40 per cent of all new loans written were coming through the broker channel and that figure is now closer to 60 per cent, which just shows how much value and trust people are beginning to place in brokers. Going forward, people are using brokers more and more, simply because the lending landscape is quite complicated. You get more service and, ultimately, better results if you work with a broker.

CHAPTER 4

Empowerment through education

INVESTING IN REAL estate is a proven strategy for creating wealth, and almost anyone can use property to improve their financial situation. But if investing in property successfully is such a sure thing, why doesn't everyone do it and why aren't all investors rich?

The answer boils down to something entirely boring and simple: education. Or in the case of investors who do not do well out of investing, a lack of education. In a nutshell, property education is the first and most important step you will take towards building your financial future.

In my view, education is so essential that it is always at the core of the initial meetings we have with our clients. The first thing we aim to do is to educate the client in terms of their finances.

Education can take many forms, and there is so much to learn, so we use our judgement to decide which areas to cover in depth. In essence, we tailor the education to the people we have sitting in front of us. There is no reason to start talking to people about hybrid trusts if it is not relevant to their situation, for example. If you give too much information, or too much education, you are wasting their time because people will not remember what is not relevant and they will lose focus on what matters.

Generally, our conversation begins in the same place, which is with these two key questions:

- What is your situation right now?
- What would you like your situation to be?

Once you understand your financial situation, you can start asking yourself questions such as:

- What are you trying to achieve?
- Why are you investing in property?
- Do you have specific financial goals, such as to build some wealth and some savings and prepare for retirement?

When I am working with clients, once I understand someone's goals and their personal financial situation, then I can start the education process. It usually begins with looking at the financial structure that could be put in place to help the client finance and build a portfolio.

So before we go into the nitty gritty of looking at how an actual property works, we first look at the structure of the finances. That education covers everything from how you can use lines of credit and offset accounts to your benefit, to how you protect yourself and your assets, and how to implement risk management.

The idea of giving you this education is to show you how all of the pieces of the puzzle work together, so you can make financial decisions from an informed place. Your first or next steps as a property investor will depend on your starting position – whether you have any savings behind you, whether you have invested before, etc. – but the process always starts with the same step.

How property works

The next part of the process, after gaining an education on the finance side of things, is to actually understand how an investment property works. The best way to do that is to go through the numbers.

Many people who are new to investing do not have an appreciation of just how much money is involved when they acquire a property. For example, for a property purchase of half a million dollars, they will need to pay approximately $20,000 in stamp duty, perhaps a sum for LMI, around $3,000 in bank fees and legal fees, and a few other expenses. That $500,000 investment ends up costing about $530,000.

Knowing how much it will cost is one thing; knowing how much money you need to get started is another.

How much money do you need to buy a $500,000 property?

Let's say you are planning to borrow 80 per cent from the bank.

This requires a deposit of 20 per cent or $100,000. Add your deposit ($100,000) to the buying costs, including stamp duty, etc. ($30,000), then you are looking at around $130,000.

These funds need to come out of your savings account, or line of credit if you have one against your own home or another investment.

So – when purchasing a $500,000 property at an 80 per cent borrowing ratio (or 'lend'), you need $130,000.

What about a 90 per cent loan?

In this case, you still need the $30,000 for buying costs, but your deposit will be lower: 90 per cent of $500,000 is $45,000, therefore you will need around $80,000. However, you may have to add LMI to this calculation as you are borrowing at a higher LVR.

Calculating these sums on potential property deals is part of the education process that you go through as you learn about investing. When you learn how to crunch these numbers 'on the fly', you become able to quickly and effectively work out what property types and deals are affordable to you and which ones are not.

This gives you the ability to be agile, flexible and, more importantly in a hot market, fast – all very meaningful qualities as a successful investor.

How much money do you need to own and manage the property?

The first part of your education will involve learning about deposits and property purchases. The next step is to ask yourself, 'what kind of cash flow can you expect from that particular property?'

With our clients, we go through comprehensive 10-year projections which outline everything from what kind of rent you can expect to receive, the formulas you can use to calculate strong yields and how to plan effective investments that far out in advance. I often talk about what I call the 'rule of one thousand' which basically means you need your weekly rent to be about one-thousandth of the purchase price.

For example, if you buy a property for $500,000, then your weekly rental income should be one-thousandth of that, which is $500, at a minimum. It is a simple rule of thumb and it is by no means the last line of defence when doing your due diligence, but it is a great method for doing quick calculations to ensure that the cash flow of a particular property is going to be acceptable.

Cash flow is just one calculation, we also discuss the following topics with our clients:

- Profit and loss calculations
- Varying returns when interest rates change (up and down)
- LVR strategy
- Funding sources for the deposit and the financial implications of each.

Finally, we review the depreciation opportunities, the client's tax situation, and we forecast what kind of tax loss they are going to make. Based on the income and tax outcomes, we can then work out what the likely tax rebate is going to be and what the weekly cash flow is going to be as a result of owning this property.

As you can see – it looks like a complicated process! But it's actually quite straightforward once you know how to do it and what the process is like. Best of all, once you know what you are doing, these steps can be replicated again and again for different property purchases and scenarios.

How do you make money out of property?

Once you have a basic education about the process of buying and managing real estate investments, you can then start to understand how you can make money out of investing.

We talk about keeping property for the long term, for 15 or 20 years if you can. From our perspective at Multifocus Properties & Finance, we believe investing happens in stages. There is the 'planning' phase, when you go through education and devise an investment strategy; this is what this very chapter is all about. Then when you are ready, you enter the 'accumulation' stage, which is when you acquire a property (or two, three, four, or however many properties are decided upon in the strategy).

Once you reach your target and you have stopped buying properties because you have got the portfolio you want, then we go into the 'transition' phase. This is also a holding or 'growth' stage, because you pretty much do nothing and just let capital growth work its magic. You then sit on your investments for 10 to 15 years.

Then, you go into the 'drawdown' phase, when you are actually cashing in your wealth so you can go happily ever after into retirement. That final phase of the process may involve selling some or all of the properties to release the gains and make some serious money out of your investments. We work with our clients to teach them a number of strategies to maximise the amount of money they make when they sell.

When I explain these phases to a client in person, I love watching them experience that moment of realisation. When we see a client for the first time they are usually saying something along the lines of, 'I want to invest in property, but I do not know what to do.' During that planning phase is where all the education comes in; without it, you are really investing in the dark, but with it you can work towards clear and exciting financial goals.

Generally speaking, when you are planning to make money out of property, you have the following three broad options at the conclusion of your investing run.

1. Sell your entire portfolio

You can sell the whole lot and enjoy a huge profit all at once – except that you have to pay a whopping CGT bill. You will also have to put the money in the bank and live off the interest, and you will no longer enjoy any growth in the property market. There is nothing wrong with paying CGT, you just have to accept that this is part of the process of realising your gains. By liquidating your portfolio and investing the proceeds in a savings account or similar, you buy yourself an income stream that is as safe as can be.

2. Aggressively pay down your loans

Once you have stopped buying properties, i.e. when you enter the 'transition' phase, your cash flow should get better and you can use some of the surplus income to repay your loans at an aggressive pace. Assuming you have paid off your own home loan already and the cash flow of your property gets better and better then, by the time you retire, the cash flow your portfolio generates is hopefully going to be enough for you to live off. At retirement age, you then do not need to do anything except enjoy your rental income – and you are still in the game for more capital gains!

3. A hybrid of option 1 and 2

The hybrid solution is to sell some of your properties to pay off the debt on the rest of them. You therefore keep part of your portfolio, live off the rent from what you have left and still enjoy the benefit of capital growth on the investments you still hold.

Which of the three options is best?

You cannot make the decision now as to what you are going to do. You need to make the decision as you go along, from the transition phase onwards, or when you retire because you do not know how your circumstances are going to evolve in the future.

What you can do is get educated about your options and take

all the right steps and precautions possible to place you in the best position for an optimal financial outcome.

As I said, my biggest pleasure is when I see people suddenly 'get it'. They see how it works, they understand how the whole thing comes together and that is when everyone gets really excited. They can see the opportunities to create solid wealth in their future!

Of course, you could skip the education and just use a buyer's agent to do the research and find you a property. But here is the reality of the situation: you give a buyer's agent some instructions. You say, 'I want a house in this price range in that area', and you pay the buyer's agent to go out there and find the property for you.

But most buyers' agents will not be able to help you with education, with a detailed strategy, with a plan for your future – in five years, 15 years and 35 years' time!

10 key elements of property investing you need to understand (before you dive into the market)

1. It is essential to know your numbers

As I mentioned, to me, investing is not about focusing on the property, it is about focusing on the numbers. You are making decisions that are quite important and have the potential to impact your whole life, so you need to know what you are doing. Getting an education and learning how the numbers are crunched is vital. Some clients say to me, 'I do not really know how it all works but I trust you to work it out for me'. I am not comfortable with that, because at the end of the day it is not my money. I see it as part of my job to make sure every one of my clients goes into property investing with their eyes wide open, which means having a solid education and an understanding of the numbers involved.

2. You must be disciplined

If you are disciplined with your money, your money will work much harder for you and will set you up for greater financial security. If you are not disciplined with your money, the good news is that it can be managed. For example, I have clients who say, 'I have got some money in an offset account but I just spend it.' I have other clients who say, 'I make sure my offset balance increases every month because that is my measure as to how much I can save'. The more successful investors are those who fall into the second category; you need to be disciplined when you invest in property, and discipline comes with understanding the numbers.

3. Emotions have no place in investing

Property investing is all about making money. It does not matter where the property is, what it looks like, what colour the carpet is, whether the kitchen is new or not… Provided the numbers work and it is appealing to tenants, you do not need to worry about how you feel about the property. A lot of people say, 'I am not sure about this place, it is far too small for me.' But you need to understand that you are not going to live in the place, so your emotional reaction to the property does not matter! The only thing that matters is the answer to this question: is it going to make money for me? Adopt that mindset and you will realise it is not about the house, it is about making money.

4. You should invest in areas with good fundamentals

Obviously, you want to buy the property type that is in the highest demand for the area you are buying in, whether it is a house or unit. But you also need to ensure that the fundamentals of the area are going to move your investment property forward financially. You sometimes see press articles debating 'houses versus units' but to me, that is not the right question to ask, because every location will have a different market. Forty years ago, a house on a big block of land might have been the safest best, but now in capital cities, apartments can be more in demand than houses. Population growth, a good local economy, a strong tenant population, these are some of the fundamentals you need to focus on, rather than just saying, 'I want to buy a house on a big block'.

5. Make your investments as passive as you can

I am not a big fan of people getting involved in their investments, as do-it-yourself (DIY) property managers for instance. You should treat your investments like a business that you manage very passively. You already have a job and a life keeping you busy, so why add extra work to your plate? Trust the property professionals who have experience, expertise and time to properly manage your investments instead. I always recommend you plan to have a passive investment system in place, rather than trying to get involved with everything, and you will enjoy property investing with less stress. After all, when you invest in shares, you do not get involved in the management of the company you invest in, do you?

6. Invest to suit your age, lifestyle and risk profile

Every person will have a number of different factors that will influence their property investing decisions. This comes back to fundamentals. If you want a safe environment to park your money, then a more traditional investment strategy might work. If you are a more experienced investor, you might want to take a gamble in a mining town – but you need to be making that decision knowing full well what the consequences might be. I had a client who was a doctor aged 61, who lost most of his share market-invested wealth in the GFC. Shortly afterwards, he invested heavily in mining towns (which were growing very fast at the time) and then he sold them all after a few years for a quick but high profit. He regained all of his lost wealth, but his strategy was very high-risk. Generally speaking, your best bet is to invest in a safer market – but ultimately, it all comes down to your age, lifestyle and risk profile.

7. Have a clear strategy before you start

It may sound obvious, but almost everyone has trouble articulating a strategy initially. To create your strategy, you need to consider things such as: what are you trying to achieve? Are you aiming to create enough wealth to retire early? Are you saving for your children's future education? To reach those goals, you need to consider your current financial limits and opportunities. You then need to consider other limits that may impact on your strategic planning, including personal circumstances such as age, lifestyle, family, debt and more. I will cover this in greater detail in Chapter 5 – it is so important to your success that it deserves a chapter all of its own.

8. Do not blindly trust others – always do your own research

You should surround yourself with qualified experts. They are going to help you fast-track your wealth creation, because you can leverage their experience and knowledge. But it is always my view that you should check whatever your 'trusted experts' recommend – not because you are overly suspicious, but simply for peace of mind. When someone recommends a particular strategy or presents a property, you should qualify for yourself that what they are saying is true and appropriate for your situation. Talk to other experts, read investment magazines, speak with your accountant, search the internet and social networks. Only once you feel 100 per cent comfortable should you make a decision to proceed.

9. Have a risk management plan

Risk management is a crucial part of the property investing process. One key part of risk management in my mind is insurance. To me, the two major risk mitigation techniques are 'buffers' and insurance. Buffers are essentially financial resources you can access should things go awry. It can be in the form of an unused line of credit or money in a savings account. Insurance is not a cost – it is an investment in your own peace of mind. Income protection insurance, for instance, does not only protect your income stream, it also protects your family. Life insurance allows your family to be financially secure if you pass away. Trauma insurance pays a lump sum if you encounter a severe unexpected health issue. And landlords, building and contents insurance covers your actual property investments. It is worth considering taking out all of the above types of insurance to manage your risk as an investor and ensure you can cover your financial obligations, no matter how your situation changes.

10. Do not believe in 'get-rich-quick' schemes

If anyone tells you that you can own 20 properties in a year, walk in the opposite direction – fast. What will create lasting wealth is time and leverage, not greed. Also be sure to observe other investors' stories with some caution. Most investment property magazines and websites feature investor testimonials, but they often do not share enough detail – such as annual income, savings for deposits, debts and other financial information – for you to understand how the investor really built their portfolio. Do not compare yourself to anyone else or worry that you are not making progress 'fast' enough. Instead, focus on your own situation and how you can get ahead and grow your own wealth as a property investor.

CHAPTER 5

Defining your investment strategy

EVERYONE WHO CHOOSES to invest in property has the same broad objective: to make money. But outside of this general goal, many investors will happily sink hundreds of thousands of dollars into investment properties without any real idea of what they are hoping to achieve.

To me, that is a little bit like taking on home repairs without knowing what you want to achieve. You know you want the house to look and perform better, but you are not sure exactly what to do. So you adopt a haphazard approach and you paint a wall here and upgrade an appliance there, doing what you can as you can afford it, hoping for the best.

That is no way to renovate – and it is definitely no way to invest.

Here is another example. Recently I decided to upgrade one of our toilets in our home. It had a very old 9L cistern, and I wanted to install a smaller 6L cistern, which is more water efficient. I thought, 'How hard can it be?' I went to the plumbing shop, bought the new smaller unit, came home and, after some frustrating efforts, I managed to install it. When I flushed the toilet it worked, but it did not do the job properly. I could not figure out what was wrong.

Eventually, I got a professional plumber in for another job and I asked him what was wrong with my toilet. 'All I have done is replace the cistern, but now it is not working properly,' I told him.

The plumber instantly spotted the problem and laughed. 'You need to change the bowl,' he told me. 'The bowl is shaped in a certain way to match perfectly with the cistern. If you have a 6L cistern and a 9L bowl, it just will not work.'

You don't say! I never suspected this would be an issue, because hey, I am not a plumber! He changed the bowl over and now the toilet works as good as new.

It was a simple DIY job, I thought, so I attempted to do it myself – but it did not work, because I did it on my own without having the necessary skills, expertise and experience.

This is exactly what it is like if you attempt to invest in property without having a clear investment strategy to guide you on every aspect of the process.

If you have a plumbing job, hire a plumber. If you are looking at investing in shares, hire a financial planner or a share broker. And if you are looking at investing in property, get a property adviser on board to help you establish and follow a tailored investment strategy. You will avoid so many mistakes if you do.

Avoiding the traps of beginner investors

I am often approached by clients who are confused about what to do. They might be first-time investors or people with a little experience in property, but the thing they have in common is that they have not yet created an investment strategy or have set themselves a plan to move forward. Clients who are in this situation are often not sure how to proceed or where they ideally want to be in the future.

They will come to me and say, 'Philippe, someone told us 'x' and someone else told us 'y', and then I go on the internet and it says something else entirely. Who is right and what should we do?'

Going back to what we have discussed in previous chapters, this really demonstrates my point about the importance of education.

It is so crucial to your success that you seek advice from people who know what they are talking about. You can talk to seasoned investors and family and friends, but if they have invested without seeking expert advice along the way, they may not actually know what they are doing, they could have just got lucky. So they could give you advice and suggestions that will not work for you and just send you down the wrong path.

However, if you get someone professional to help you out, it will assist you to cut through a lot of clutter and confusion and avoid making the mistakes that can cost other investors a lot of money.

The very first thing that people can do to avoid the traps often encountered by beginner investors therefore is to gather the right people around them. A good property adviser, a good mortgage broker, a good conveyancer and a good accountant are the people you ideally want on your investment team.

The next thing you can do is to commit to your own education. Education comes in all forms, such as reading books and magazines, going to seminars and browsing the internet for resources. Then, once something comes up that you do not fully understand, you can share that question or concern with your brains trust and get some answers to your questions.

Talking to different people about your investment goals will also expose you to all different kinds of strategies. For example, I personally lean towards investing in new properties because of the depreciation benefits, but some people might prefer a renovation strategy to manufacture growth. Talking to different people will give you many ideas about different strategies you can use to maximise your situation.

One essential point you need to keep in mind is that your strategy will change over time, so it is important to review your strategy, initially on a monthly basis, then quarterly, then half-yearly, then annually, just to make sure you are not falling off the path you have set for yourself. I tend to review my strategy every year around Christmas time when everyone is on holidays and it is quiet. I sit down and go through what I have done, where I am going, whether I am on track and assess what changes I need to make to meet my goals.

A lot of things change in life and sometimes you will be working towards achieving one goal, only to realise that you actually want to reach a different goal altogether. You could be marching towards your ideal future as a single investor when the next thing you know you find a great partner, get married, have babies… and the whole plan changes.

This is not a bad thing – it is part of life. But it does mean your strategy may need to change to adapt to your new lifestyle. For example, instead of buying two properties a year for five years, you might only buy one property a year. If your financial situation changes in a positive way, you may consider riskier but more lucrative development projects. The most important thing is to ensure your strategy adapts with you as your lifestyle changes.

Four key pillars to build your investment strategy

At Multifocus Property & Finance we have devised a process for building a simple, clear and strong investment strategy and it revolves around the following four key pillars:

1. Objectives
2. Boundaries
3. Legal framework
4. Financial structure.

Let's consider each of these below.

1. Objectives

The first thing we do when we talk to new clients is to ask them why they want to invest in real estate in the first place.

Most people have answers like, 'I do not want to retire on the pension; I want to live a comfortable life rather than scraping by on two-minute noodles.' The government pension is fairly abysmal; it is presently around $21,000 a year for a couple, or $400 per week. I have not spoken to anyone who is satisfied with this as their superannuation balance and believes, 'Yes, this will be enough to allow me to live comfortably'.

It is no surprise then that many people are interested in supplementing their pension and/or superannuation with another stream of retirement income. Investing in property is a very successful way of boosting your wealth and supplementing your income when you leave the workforce.

Everyone has a different reason for wanting to invest in property. Some people want to create wealth for their children, or to fund a happy retirement, or they want to be able to retire sooner.

Of course in terms of objectives, there are also those people who come to us saying they want to invest in property so that in three years' time they can retire from their job and quit the workforce for good. These are the people who generally have no understanding whatsoever of what they are doing, because they think the rent will give them enough cash flow to replace their income – but they forget that there will still be a significant debt against the house in three years' time. Again, it is a matter of educating them and showing them that they just cannot do that.

People ultimately need to be focused on where they are going, where their investment strategy will ultimately lead them, and they should have clear objectives.

When considering your own objectives, it is helpful to ask yourself the following questions:

- What is my ultimate goal as an investor?
- How old am I and when do I want to retire from the workforce?
- How many years of 'active investing' do I have ahead of me?
- What is my risk profile?
- How many properties would I be comfortable owning?

2. Boundaries

It is important to understand your boundaries because they are what dictate how fast you can go when you want to build your investment portfolio.

Boundaries are pretty much defined by the banks. In the case of boundaries, lenders will look at two criteria: your borrowing capacity (what your income will support) and your capacity to pay a deposit (cash or equity in an existing property). You need to satisfy both to get a loan.

When I first started investing, I was an expat living in Australia on a temporary visa but, because I had a very good job and some savings behind me, I could buy some properties straight away. You may find you are in a similar, good position and you are able to get started immediately. Or you might have some work to do before you can buy. By establishing your boundaries, you will learn where your starting position is.

To establish your boundaries, you need to look at what you can actually feasibly do today, which involves the process of defining the limits of your capacity. This is all about being realistic yet ambitious. For instance, there is a lot of money to be made in subdivision and development: if you have the risk appetite for it, you can make six-figure sums in a very short space of time. But you need to have a lot of cash or equity behind you in order to take on a development project, and you have to be prepared for the risk that you may not make the profit you were projecting.

You would also be wise to have some experience as a property investor before you consider such an aggressive strategy. So while this type of investment could be a huge 'money spinner', it may not be achievable within your boundaries.

When working out your boundaries, you should go through the process of finding out what your borrowing capacity is and what deposit you can provide. You can do this in consultation with an experienced investment-focused mortgage broker. They will work through your income and debt situation, your risk profile and limitations, to create a clear picture of your boundaries.

The whole point of establishing boundaries is to show you exactly what you can and cannot do moving forward. There is no point saying, 'We are going to buy two properties each year for the next five years if your borrowing capacity is only $300,000.

Knowing your boundaries can also empower you as it helps you move into a position where you can make smart, strategic investment decisions. For example, if you know you are very restricted and your boundaries are very tight, then you can start to look at options to overcome these issues.

Let's say your serviceability is very low. You might then partner with a member of your family as a joint venture, or look at opportunities to get a job with a better salary, or consider how you might negotiate a pay rise or promotion. All of these options would improve your income and therefore improve your serviceability – allowing you to put yourself in a position where you can achieve your objectives. Conversely, if your savings are low, you need to work on a savings plan to improve your cash situation and be in a position to invest.

3. Legal framework

When I talk about your legal framework I am essentially talking about who is going to legally own the property. If you are part of a couple, legal ownership of the property may be an even division between both parties – or it could be owned in one person's name only. The ideal ownership position is going to depend on who earns the most money, who is in the highest tax bracket and who has got the longest time left in the workforce.

For example, if a young couple wishes to invest and they both earn $100,000 a year, then they could decide on a legal framework that involves a 50/50 ownership structure. But if they decide to have children, there may be two or three years when mum or dad stays at home without earning an income. That parent is potentially going to lose out on receiving tax rebates, if they are not paying income tax. In your own situation, if the intention is for someone to stay at home and raise the kids for a prolonged period of time, then it may make more sense to have the property in the name of the person who will remain employed in the workforce.

> **Did you know?**
> If an investor is not working for a while, tax deductions are not lost. They are just carried forward until the investor starts working again and then they can be offset against income taxes.

Alternatively, if there are no kids in the picture but one partner is earning $200,000 per year and the other is earning $80,000, then you would be more likely to buy the property in the name of the person earning the highest salary. This allows you to leverage greater tax deductions.

There are also issues of asset protection to consider. If you are working in a profession where you are at risk of getting sued – such as a surgeon or builder – you may want to purchase your property within a trust to protect your assets. In my view, trusts are generally not necessary for 99 per cent of the population, although this is a discussion for you to have with your accountant or financial planner.

4. Financial structure

The final piece of the puzzle when creating your investment strategy is to consider the ideal financial structure. This is highly dependent on each investor's personal situation.

The classic financial structure that most couples are familiar with is when the couple owns their own home and they want to use equity to invest in property. The financial structure for optimal success in this situation involves releasing equity in the home and segregating those funds in a separate loan split, so you can easily identify what is tax deductible and what is not.

Typically, the way you extract equity for this purpose is by setting up a line of credit and the line of credit is generally fully transactional. This means that all of your property expenses and rental income would be deposited and withdrawn from this account when you need it.

Many people use their line of credit purely for their investment properties and then use an offset account on their home loan for private expenses such as paying bills and buying groceries.

Someone who has not got a home loan or a property to leverage against will need to use savings to put down a deposit. The optimal financial structure for this scenario is often the strategic use of an offset account but, again, it depends on your specific situation and your boundaries.

There are many options available to borrowers and I have only touched on a few of them in this book. The ultimate goal as an investor is to minimise your interest payable and maximise your money in the most tax-efficient way possible. For this reason, we discuss various finance strategies with our clients in great detail to ensure they select the most suitable financial structure for their situation.

What are the risks of investing without a clear strategy?

It all boils down to this: if you do not have a plan and you do things without understanding the numbers, the real risk is that you will buy the wrong property in the wrong place.

Investing without having a clear strategy exposes you to risks such as:

- Being unable to resell the property for a profit

- Failing to recover a profit after renovating
- Doing the wrong types of renovations and decreasing the property's appeal
- Failing to make money out of your investment because you bought in the wrong location, and the list goes on!

These are just some of the risks you are taking when you rush into property investing without having a structured plan to guide your decisions.

I remember a few years ago, I met a pilot who worked for one of the big Australian airlines and he had a property in Moranbah, Queensland. I talked to him about updating his strategy to broaden his asset base and buy a property in a capital city. He was a very busy man so he wanted a passive investment strategy. I suggested we look at Sydney, Brisbane or Melbourne, and he said, 'But the yields are terrible compared to Moranbah.' 'Yes that is true,' I replied. 'But Moranbah is a mining town and you need to diversify your risk.'

Keep in mind that at the time he had a property for which he paid $400,000 and he was receiving a rental income of $3,000 per week! And here I was, advising him to invest in a capital city where he would pay $500,000 for a property and achieve just $500 a week rent.

Obviously, it was very hard to convince him not to buy another property in Moranbah. He was very close to doing so, but in the end he bought one of the properties I advised him on. Now when we talk, he says he is so glad he listened to me and did not invest in another Moranbah property.

Many of you will know that the property bubble did burst in Moranbah, as mining projects came to an end. Values fell by 80 per cent off from their peaks in 2011 to 2013 and, by 2016, it was virtually impossible to find tenants or sell property in that market.

Today, my client's Moranbah property is dragging down his overall portfolio as it has put a huge dampener on his serviceability. He has a huge debt on the property and it is not rented out. Luckily he is an airline pilot and he earns a very good salary so he can cope but, going forward, every strategy we put together, we have to factor in coping with that Moranbah property.

Mining towns can serve their purpose for a short period of time, but investing in these areas is a very risky strategy, particularly if you are not thinking ahead. This is why it is so important to have a strategy in place because it gives you a clear path to follow and you can make smart decisions that impact your future in a positive way.

How to invest successfully in any market

Invest in strong locations. This means locations with population growth, good infrastructure and a population base that is large enough to generate new infrastructure. In my opinion, you need a population of at least 200,000 to sustain the type of vibrant and growing community that will underpin long-term capital growth. Any fewer than 200,000 people and I would be cautious to invest.

Always diversify. Do not buy the same property type in the same location, over and over again. Buy a mix of apartments, townhouses and houses in different locations. Every location in Australia has a different market cycle and they are always at different phases of their cycle. Buying properties across the board spreads your risk so that while one area is in a slow phase, another is booming.

Have financial buffers in place. There is no point investing every last cent you have in your property investments; if you do, you leave yourself terribly exposed to financial hardship if anything even slightly unexpected happens. Ideally, you want to have a line of credit available to absorb any financial emergencies related to your investments, or, at the very least, make sure you have plenty of savings or equity in your home.

STAGE 2: ACCUMULATION

Finding proven property performers

HERE IS THE truth of the matter: if you do not achieve growth in your property portfolio then you are simply wasting your time.

I field enquiries all the time from investors who want to know, 'How can I find a positive cash flow property investment?' I can understand the appeal of a property that generates an instant profit, but you have to think about the bigger picture; it may put $50 back in your pocket each week now, but how is that going to make you wealthy?

To create lasting wealth that sustains you for many years in retirement, you need to invest in quality properties that grow in value over time. This means that during your accumulation phase, you must seek out proven property performers that are most likely to appreciate in value.

The accumulation phase of your investing journey is where, funnily enough, you accumulate all the properties you need to reach your target. In my view, you should aim to do that as quickly and efficiently as possible, so you can enjoy the longest period of growth.

One part of the accumulation phase that investors need to get their head around is the fact that during this time you tend not to build up too much equity. Every time you do create equity, you will extract it to get into your next property, so during this period it may seem like you are not making much progress regarding your overall wealth.

This is all part of the process; the accumulation phase is the busiest, most costly part of property investing, but it is also brief. Sometimes it can be as short as one or two years, and other times up to 10 years or more, depending on your situation.

Consider it this way: if you accumulate five properties in your portfolio in three years, you may then hold those properties for 20 years and enjoy two decades of property price growth.

If you buy one property every four years, you are still going to end up with five properties in retirement. But you will not benefit from those many years of value appreciation, so your wealth position will be somewhat lower. For these reasons, my advice is to create a plan and then buy as many properties as you can, as fast as you can (taking into account your income and risk profile).

Of course, if you are buying the wrong types of properties, then it is not going to matter how many you buy or how quickly you buy them! They will not create wealth for you.

That is why this section of the book deals with educating you about finding proven property performers. I am going to show you all of the steps required to find good quality, high growth properties that will move your portfolio forward – and ideally, deliver you to an abundant retirement.

CHAPTER 6

Designing your ultimate portfolio

I HAVE LEARNT many things about property investing over the years, but one aspect of owning real estate that I know to be true beyond any doubt is this: the most successful property investors are those who have a plan.

Ultimately, property values always increase in value. They may not increase in value in a linear fashion – a property may grow in value one year and decrease in value the next – but over the long term, property prices always go up eventually.

Let's consider Sydney property prices over the last few decades to illustrate this point further.

In 1970, the median house price in Sydney was just over $18,000.[1]

By 1980 it had almost quadrupled to $68,000.

---

1 Source: *Housing Prices In Australia: 1970 to 2003*
(www.econ.mq.edu.au/Econ_docs/research_papers2/2004_research_papers/Abelson_9_04.pdf)q

By 1990 it had tripled again to $194,000.

The year 2000 saw median property prices in Sydney reach $287,000.

By 2010, house prices were well over half a million dollars – and we all know what happened from there.

If you were an investor in the 1980s, and you had purchased 10 properties over that period for less than $100,000 each, you would now have a property portfolio worth more than $10 million. How does that sound? Wouldn't that provide a comfortable retirement?

The purpose behind designing your ultimate property portfolio is to make a clear plan now for the future, so you can one day be one of those people who looks back and says, 'Remember when you could buy property in Sydney for less than $2 million? Thank goodness I bought five of them when I could afford it!'

The purpose behind your property investments

To create your ideal property portfolio, it is important to start with your retirement goal and work backwards from there when creating your investment strategy.

The reality for most people is that our superannuation is not going to get us where we want to be in terms of financial comfort and security – and yes, even wealth – in retirement.

Many of us are not even sure how much income we will need in retirement or how many investment properties that equates to. So, when planning for your financially abundant future, you really need a clear idea of where you stand right now. I generally suggest to my clients that they should see a financial planner and get an understanding of the numbers.

Work out your superannuation situation precisely with a financial planner and be sure to consider the following:

- How much money you have in your superannuation today
- How much money you are likely to contribute to your superannuation throughout the rest of your career
- How much money you should salary sacrifice, if possible/relevant, to increase your superannuation balance
- How much money you want to live on, each year, when you retire.

With all of this information, your financial planner can calculate how much you are likely to be living off in retirement, based on your current superannuation and investments. They will adjust the balance for inflation and then work back to today's numbers. This will give you a clear idea of the gap between where you are right now and where you would like to be.

Let's say your financial planner's modelling reveals that you will be living off around $50,000 per year (in today's dollars) in retirement. However, you wish to travel, explore and enjoy your retirement years, so you would prefer to live off $100,000 in retirement.

By doing very simplistic calculations, assuming a 5 per cent per annum return on investment, I can estimate that to retire on $100,000 per year in today's money you need around $2 million in super. This is assuming that you are not going to eat into your capital base, which is the $2 million itself. Once you start chipping away at these funds, it means that at some point you are going to run out of money.

Now, if you have $1 million in a superannuation account and your super fund returns around 5 per cent per annum, you are only going to have $50,000 per year to live off. The gap between where you are headed now in retirement ($50,000) and where you want to be ($100,000) is $50,000 per year. To fund your lifestyle at $100,000, you will either have to eat into the capital of your super or supplement your retirement income with property.

In this scenario, if I very simplistically translate that into properties, you will need a $1 million property portfolio (in today's money) free and clear in retirement to fund the $50,000 shortfall.

To hedge against lower returns and unexpected expenses, let's aim for $2 million in property assets on top of your superannuation balance. If you are buying properties priced at around $500,000, you will need four unencumbered properties to sustain your retirement, bringing you a rental income after expenses of around 5 per cent.

These are all very crude calculations, but they give you an understanding of how you can start the process of calculating your ultimate property portfolio.

A number of years ago I saw a report by Ross Greenwood, the finance expert from Channel 9. Funnily enough, Ross shared a similar point of view when he said that when you retire, you would need four properties to sustain your lifestyle: one to live in, one to pay your taxes and two to provide you with an income.

The right number of properties for you may not be four; it will depend on a number of variables. We go through a detailed questionnaire with our clients to come up with an ideal number of investment properties to work towards that suits their situation.

The calculations required to come up with your ultimate goal are also quite complicated because within your super fund there are countless rules and regulations (which are always changing), including concessional tax rules that can save you a lot of money. This is why it is important to work with a financial planner, so you can optimise your money now and in retirement.

You can create ballpark figures to create your goals. The process for designing your ultimate property portfolio is always the same. You must start by considering the following questions:

- How much money do you want to retire on?
- How much will your superannuation fund cover?
- How many properties do you need to own to cover the rest?

I know how many properties I need... What next?

Designing your ultimate property portfolio is the 'theory' side of the equation. To put that theory into practice you actually need to start investing in property, which requires you to take action.

This can be quite a complicated emotional journey when you are starting out, which is what led me to create my business as a multi-step support service. From strategy and finance to property selection, we work with our clients every step of the way to make sure they are making educated and informed decisions that will move their financial situation forward, rather than getting them stuck.

Let's go back to our earlier example and assume that you are looking to eventually own four unencumbered properties worth about $2 million, which will deliver an annual income in retirement of $100,000.

The next thing you want to know is: how do I reach retirement with these properties unencumbered – in other words, fully paid off?

1. Buy properties, sooner rather than later

You need to jump into the market and start buying properties. And you need to buy properties as quickly as possible, because time in the market is what delivers the most capital growth. The more time you have until retirement, the more time your portfolio has to accumulate value.

The pace at which you acquire property will depend on your personal circumstances. In my case, coming off the back of working at a great company as an expat and enjoying a strong, stable salary for a number of years, I was in a position where I could buy several properties straight away. I bought seven properties in six months, simply because I was in the position to do so.

If you do not have enough equity or borrowing capacity to take such drastic action so quickly, that does not need to hold you back. You can still build your portfolio without stretching your finances by adding new investments to your portfolio as and when you can afford to.

2. Do not rush

Yes, it is important to buy as soon as possible so you can have time in the market – but the last thing you want to do is over-commit your finances. If you are in a position where you can buy one property comfortably but two properties would be a stretch, then I would advise you to just buy one property. You can wait a little until your situation improves and you are not going to be under financial pressure for your next investment. Remember, investing in property is a long-haul strategy, not a get-rich-quick scheme.

3. Use equity to your advantage

In the accumulation phase of your journey, adding to your portfolio should be quite a stress-free process. As we mentioned earlier, every time you get some equity in a property, try to release that equity to pay the deposit on the next property. By doing this, you will not really build equity in your overall portfolio because every time you experience growth you are using it to buy the next property. But this is a short-term phase lasting only a few years. Once you have bought the number of properties that you have planned to, you stop accessing equity, you stop buying and then the capital growth keeps growing.

This is where your equity starts building up. You need your capital gains to outgrow your debt in order to create wealth, which means selecting the right properties in locations where there is good capital growth.

4. Wait for capital gains

Once your accumulation phase is over, you will be into the next phase of investing, which we call the transition phase. In other words, you just wait for capital gains to work its magic.

It might be a good idea to start slowly repaying some of that debt during this phase, but not before paying off your own home loan as your first priority, because your home loan is not tax deductible.

Once you have repaid your home loan, you have rid yourself of your 'bad debt'. If you are lucky enough to have plenty of time ahead of you (i.e. you are around 25 to 30 years from retirement), then you can allow for your rental income and salary to pay off the majority of your investment home loans. However, in many instances, it is a good idea to start repaying your investment mortgages during the transition phase so by the time you retire your properties are either substantially or fully paid off.

If you have a smaller investment timeline ahead of you, such as 10 to 20 years, then you might want to sell one or two properties upon retirement, so you can use the proceeds to reduce the debt on the rest of the portfolio. These are some of the calculations you will need to make when you get to that point in your life.

You do not need to make these decisions on your own, however. Talk to a financial planner, a financial adviser, your accountant, and/or your property advisers. You will get a range of opinions about what you can do and where you are heading, and then you can make some informed decisions. Education and self-awareness is key here: at the end of the day, it is your money and nobody can or should make these decisions for you.

Aggressive or passive buying strategy: which is best?

Deciding just how passive or aggressive you need to be when designing your ultimate property portfolio depends on a number of factors, the most important of which is often your age.

If you are a brand new investor aged 20 to 25 years old, then you have at least 30 years ahead of you until retirement, depending on your goals. This is a really strong position to be in, in terms of time in the market.

However, the sticking point for young people is often their deposit (or lack thereof). How many twenty-somethings do you know who have a spare $100,000 lying around to use as a property deposit? Some are in the fortunate position of having parents who are willing to help their kids get on the property ladder, but others will need to save for a period of time to get their property deposit together.

Either way, an investor in their twenties has a lot of time ahead of them, so they can afford to take a more passive approach to investing in property. It can be slow going at the beginning and they still need a clear strategy to guide them forward, but they do not need to be aggressive in order to create a wealthy retirement.

At the other end of the spectrum is someone aged 55 years or over who is getting close to retirement age, and they suddenly realise they only have $300,000 in superannuation – which will not be enough to sustain them for two or three decades after they stop working. For these people, there is a sense of urgency. Their exact investment strategy will depend on their individual circumstances, but someone aged in their mid-fifties will need to adopt more aggressive methods of investing, such as joint ventures.

This was the case with one of my clients, aged in his early fifties when we met. He had a wife and five children. He was a senior executive in a company and he made a great living. He also had plenty of equity in his home.

However, with such a big family to take care of, and a very low-risk profile due to a conservative upbringing, he had never invested in anything other than a modest share portfolio. He is only now, on the advice of his financial planner, realising that he should be diversifying by investing in property.

Because of his age and his limited investment timeline, we worked out that he needed to start investing in a hurry, by adopting quite an aggressive investment strategy. Fortunately, he was in the position where he could afford to buy up to four properties immediately so he was able to dramatically transform his situation quite quickly.

An aggressive approach can help you in acquiring more properties more quickly, but it is not appropriate in every situation. For example, I recently met a single mother with two children. She has a great, stable job and earns a $100,000 annual salary, but receives no financial support from the children's father. She would like to be very aggressive because she wants to secure her financial future. Right now she has got enough savings and is in a strong enough income position to support two investment properties.

But my advice to her was to go and see a financial planner, slow down and not to use all of her savings. She is a single mother with the responsibility of two young preschool-aged children; she needs a financial buffer to help her in case of life's little emergencies, rather than over-committing and putting her own home at risk due to being too aggressive.

Ultimately the right approach, whether aggressive or passive, comes down to finding a balance that you are comfortable with. With the right financial structure in place, a risk minimisation plan and a clear investment strategy, you can invest confidently and sleep at night, knowing you are not in danger of running out of money any time soon.

Balancing cash flow with capital growth

I have talked a lot about the number of properties you need to own in your portfolio, but I have not yet gone into too much detail about the types of properties you should buy.

The story of cash flow versus capital gains is a classic one; you often read in property magazines or on websites about the pros and cons of each strategy. However, this is the wrong debate to be having. It is assumed that if you go for capital gains properties, your cash flow is going to be negative, and if you go for cash flow positive properties your capital gains are going to be nonexistent. Furthermore, when talking about 'cash flow positive' properties, are you talking about cash flow positive before tax or after tax? Let's clarify what we are talking about.

For the vast majority of investors, i.e. those borrowing 80 to 90 per cent of the property purchase price, a cash flow positive property before tax is almost impossible to find – unless you are investing in a 'thriving' mining town (and how long will that last?). For these investors, most properties only become cash flow positive after tax deductions and depreciation take effect.

So, we are actually talking about using negative gearing to allow your property to become cash flow positive. This is the sweet spot to be in.

There is no question in my mind that the name of the game is capital growth. If you do not have capital growth, you are wasting your time. If you buy cash flow positive properties that have limited growth potential, then they might put $2,000 or $3,000 a year into your pocket, but that is loose change compared to the $25,000 growth per year you could have on a $500,000 property that experiences capital growth of 5 per cent in the first couple of years.

You are talking about a few thousand dollars in cash flow versus $25,000 in capital gains – to me there is no contest there! Capital gains are what you want.

However, that said, you need to protect yourself when you buy for capital gain. You need a strong cash flow to help you maintain your investments for the long term. So while you should aim for capital growth investment, you also need to watch your cash flow.

I will give you an example. I recently saw a one-bedroom apartment for sale for $750,000 (you guessed it, it was in Sydney!). The rent was only $530 a week. By doing basic calculations, I worked out that this probably would cost the investor around $250 a week... after tax.

If you are a high-income earner you might be thinking, 'I can cope with $250 a week'. And you might well be able to. But what happens when interest rates go up 1 per cent, or 2 per cent, or more? Then you would be suddenly paying $400 or $500 a week out of your own pocket for one property. How are you going to cope with that?

And what happens if you have a portfolio of properties? What if you are not talking about just one property at that level, but four or five properties? At some point your finances are going to fall apart.

To minimise the risk of this happening, you need to achieve a balance between capital growth and yield.

Coming back to my rule of one thousand, if you are buying a $500,000 property, you want your rent to be at least one thousandth of the price per week. If you are looking at buying an apartment for $750,000, then you want the rent to be at least $750 per week to make it sustainable. If you're only getting $530 in rent per week, you are in the danger zone.

By following the rule of one thousand and having other risk management strategies in place, such as cash buffers, then you can usually fairly easily ride out any cash flow constraints if and when interest rates do increase.

CHAPTER 7

Choosing the right property

BY NOW YOU might be thinking that you are half-way into a book about successful property investing, and I have barely talked about property yet. Do not be confused: this is intentional! Property selection is crucially important to your wealth creation success but, as you have hopefully learned by now, it is not the only thing that matters. Rather, it is one small step in your overall investment strategy.

So far, I have discussed all of the important fundamentals of finance and strategy that you need to get right before you start buying property.

Now, I am going to dive into the fundamentals of property selection, to help you discover the difference between an average property and a proven property performer. When selecting an investment property, it is important to consider the following factors:

- **Location** – this is definitely the main driver of capital growth; so what constitutes an A-list location and where can these properties be found?

- **Infrastructure** – what does 'infrastructure' mean and what should you look for as an investor?
- **Property condition** – should you be adding established, new or near-new homes to your portfolio?
- **Balance** – how do you strike a balance between yield and capital growth?
- **Property cycle** – timing the market is ideal, but how do you confidently buy at the bottom of the market cycle?
- **Point of difference** – how can you ensure your investment property stands out from the rest?

Location

There are a lot of things you can change about a property: its layout, its condition, its colour, even the number of bedrooms. What you cannot ever change is its location so it is essential that you do your research to get this right from the very beginning.

If you do not buy in the right location, you run the risk of experiencing a lack of price appreciation and inconsistent rental income. In a nutshell, this means less capital growth and less cash flow – both of which are essential to grow wealth.

When we are sourcing properties for our clients, we start by talking directly to the experts who are in various markets across Australia – such as Tim Lawless, Director of Research at Corelogic, who has been specialising in real estate markets and demographic trends for many years – to find out where the profitable locations are.

So what should you be looking for in terms of location? There are a number of key factors, including:

- **Sizeable, growing population.** I would generally recommend towns with at least 200,000 people. You also

want evidence showing that the population is growing, because that is what drives jobs and the economy.
- **Strong economy.** I call this the 'pillars of economy', which means that there are several pillars or industries supporting the local economy. If there is a town relying solely on one industry for employment, then that is a huge risk. I prefer to look at areas that have several sources of employment.
- **Historical market performance.** When you have locked down a location with a good population, a growing population and a strong economy, you then need to look at the performance of the market. Where is the area in its market cycle? Is it on an upwards swing or is it trending down?
- **Lifestyle considerations.** Properties close to amenities, restaurants, nightlife, or natural attractions such as beaches and bushland should not be ignored.

Once you have located your broader suburb based on the above, you will then zoom into what type of investment is best in that area: an apartment or a house? This will be deduced by your research. For instance, if a city is experiencing an over-supply of apartments, then you may want to focus on houses in that area.

To summarise, when you are deciding upon the location of your next investment property, what you are looking to do is to ensure that all the fundamentals for growth are present.

When we are sourcing locations for our clients, our goal is generally to source locations that have not been in the media yet, so we can be ahead of the curve. Once an area is in the media it is often too late, because by then the market has moved substantially and may be reaching its peak in the cycle.

Infrastructure

Infrastructure is a major consideration when you are working out where to invest. Technically, looking for infrastructure is part of your 'location hunting' process, but it is so important, I decided it needed its own category.

When talking about infrastructure in a property investment sense, I am referring to any kind of infrastructure – generally in transport, but also in industry or retail – that will benefit local residents. This could be anything from a new train line or expanded freeway, to commercial construction that adds employment opportunities to the region.

If you have got housing nearby and a large infrastructure project is concluded, the housing will usually benefit in terms of increased access to amenities and an increase in property price growth.

I have seen bridges built across a river, which have made properties more accessible, and therefore property prices went up. I have seen a train station and new rail lines being built and, when the station opened, surrounding property prices increased.

A good example of this is the suburb of Springfield, west of Brisbane. We looked at some stock back in 2012 when local property prices were very affordable. Because Springfield was around an hour's drive from Brisbane at the time, it was not an easily commutable distance to the city and it lacked some appeal to those who worked in the city.

We were sourcing house and land packages on behalf of our clients for around $380,000. These were brand new four-bedroom homes on large blocks of land, so at this price they presented good value. They were also renting for around $380 to $400 per week, which fell within my 'rule of one thousand' philosophy.

At the time, they were building a rail line in between Springfield and the Brisbane CBD to reduce the commute time. You could see it being built and you could see the train station, which had been constructed but was not yet in use. The imminent arrival of new infrastructure was obvious. But because it was not working yet, property prices did not move.

In December 2013 when the train station opened, the commute between Springfield and Brisbane reduced considerably. You can now manage the journey by train in 29 to 36 minutes. As a result, the area suddenly became much more appealing. Demand increased and prices for family homes quickly shot up to around $450,000.

Our clients who had purchased in Augustine Heights (near Springfield) under our advice were thrilled: their investments enjoyed capital growth of $80,000 in the space of 18 months!

So as you can see, infrastructure is very important. It could be bridges, it could be train lines, it could be a new shopping complex that delivers thousands of jobs to the area. Anything that makes people move faster to their place of work, or improves their access to employment, is key.

Property condition

When deciding which property to invest in, you have a few basic options: buy new, buy old, renovate and sell, renovate and keep. When taking into account your investment strategy, there is always a debate about which of the above options is best. The right answer will depend on a number of factors, including your personal strategy and your goals, but here is my two cents on the subject in a broad sense.

As I have mentioned earlier in this book, investing in property is a financial decision. It is not about property – it is about making money. I also recognise that most of us are busy people. We have careers, businesses, relationships, children, hobbies and other obligations. So why add to the pile by making your property investments yet another thing vying for your attention?

Rather, for most of our clients, we encourage a passive investment strategy. The idea is to make your wealth creation strategy as passive as possible. Have a property manager to manage it for you; have an accountant to take care of the tax reporting for you; have insurance to manage the risk for you; have a mortgage broker to manage your loans for you.

It is not quite 'set and forget', but it is 'set and have as little to do with it as possible'. If your investments are set up and managed properly in the first place, your portfolio should tick along.

Setting all of that aside, let's touch on tax briefly. Most property investors have to earn some kind of a wage so they can benefit from negative gearing.

If you buy a brand new property for $400,000, you might generate a $3,000 or $4,000 cash loss before tax each year. But when you factor in depreciation on a new property, which I will talk more about in Chapter 9, your on-paper loss could be as high as $15,000 to $20,000 worth of taxable losses.

If you are paying between 35 to 50 per cent tax, $15,000 to $20,000 is a decent deduction as it puts between $5,000 and $10,000 back in your bank account each financial year. This more than offsets your loss before tax of $3,000 to $4,000, which is why depreciation is a very powerful tool to improve your cash flow.

Now, let's assume that you bought an older property instead, one which generated very little by way of depreciation. The equation is very different, because you are looking at a depreciation deduction of maybe $2,000 or $3,000. Combined with your real loss, you may be able to deduct around $5,000 to $7,000. After tax, your property is cash flow negative. See Table 7.1 below for calculations at the tax rate of 37 per cent plus 2 per cent Medicare Levy Surcharge and Table 7.2 at a tax rate of 45 per cent plus 2 per cent Medicare Levy Surcharge and 2 per cent Repair Levy Surcharge.

Table 7.1: Investor cash flow: 39 per cent tax rate

	New property	Old property
Real cash loss per year	$4,000	$4,000
Depreciation	$11,000	$2,000
Total tax deduction	$15,000	$6,000
Tax refund at around 39 per cent	$5,850	$2,340
Cash flow per year (tax refund – real loss)	$1,850	-$1,660

Table 7.2: Investor cash flow: 49 per cent tax rate

	New property	Old property
Real cash loss per year	$4,000	$4,000
Depreciation	$11,000	$2,000
Total tax deduction	$15,000	$6,000
Tax refund at around 49 per cent	$7,350	$2,940
Cash flow per year (tax refund – real loss)	$3,350	-$1,060

* Tax rates current as of 2016. 2 per cent Temporary Budget Repair Levy also applied from 1 July 2014 to the 2014-15, 2015-16 and 2016-17 financial years.

So which one do you want?

To summarise, we have a philosophy that suggests passive investing is the easiest path towards property wealth and it's essential that you have an understanding of how depreciation can boost your cash flow.

We can also take into consideration that with a newer property, you are not very likely to experience as many repairs and maintenance issues, because everything is brand new. With these understandings, a new property starts to make a lot of sense as a preferred investment choice.

That is not to say there is anything wrong with buying an older property and renovating; you just have to be very careful about what you are doing. You may buy an old house and plan to do a cosmetic renovation, but when you start the refurbishment you realise the plumbing is shot and suddenly your budget blows out. There are many risks with a renovation strategy and you need to consider all of them before going down this path.

Personally, I would be incapable of doing any kind of renovation; I am completely useless with my hands! Therefore, I would have to hire tradies and all the profit of renovating would flow back to them. I would also have to manage them, which I do not have time for.

Buying old and renovating is a good strategy for people who are in the trade and who know what they are doing. But if you are a white-collar worker like myself, I would think twice before investing in an older home to renovate for profit. Why take this risk, when a much simpler, easier and more profitable option is available?

Balance

Finding the ideal investment property is about finding balance. Many people will debate whether you should invest in capital growth versus cash flow properties, but in my view that is the wrong thing to ask – because you ultimately need both for your investment to succeed.

As we said earlier, the key is to find a balance between capital growth and cash flow. Having said that, you need to be careful of your cash flow, because a lack of cash flow can impact your ability to borrow and grow your portfolio.

As an example of the risks of investing purely with capital growth as your focus, if you buy a growth property in a capital city suburb, the yield can be very low.

The property might cost you $700,000, but the return is just $500 per week, falling well short of my 'rule of one thousand'.

In today's dollars, that property is going to cost you at least $250 a week to own after rent and tax, which will make your property very cash flow negative. If interest rates increase by 1 or 2 per cent you have got an even bigger problem, because you are then looking at a $400 or $450 a week negative cash flow.

This is a huge financial risk to take as it equates to more than $20,000 per year you are losing on your property investment. You would want to be pretty darn certain that its capital growth is very strong!

As a guide, one way to achieve balance is to stick to the middle ground in a given suburb. Do not buy property that is too cheap, do not buy property that is too expensive; just look for the median and aim to buy at around that price point. When you purchase a property in the middle of the market, you give your investment the biggest chance of appealing to the broadest section of the population.

Property cycle

Wherever you are planning to invest, part of your due diligence process should be to discover where that particular location is in the property cycle. Herron Todd White is an excellent resource for this information because they publish free, monthly property cycle reports outlining exactly where each major regional and capital city in Australia is at in their market cycle (see www.htw.com.au).

It is important to understand that property cycles do not go in a straight line upwards. The typical property cycle is flat for five years – sometimes even longer – which is generally followed by a big growth spike for two to three years, before the market goes flat again.

A logical pattern of growth is outlined in the list below:

- Balanced supply and demand in a market = property values that do not move.
- Population growth begins to surge and fuels the market = strong demand.
- Demand outstrips supply and puts pressure on the market = property values increase.
- Construction levels pick up. Builders and developers overshoot the market and too much stock is released = oversupply dragging down the market and flat growth.

Note that rental yields lag property prices in the surge phase, but tend to catch up once property prices flatten out.

Sometimes in a property market that has boomed too strongly, there is a correction. Sometimes there is a large correction, if the market has experienced a lot of volatility. But overall, the above pattern of growth tends to play out across the country in different ways.

> Long periods of flat growth when the market is balanced →
> Short bursts of growth when demand outstrips supply →
> Rebalance is restored, and the market goes flat again.

The optimal time to buy as an investor is clearly at the bottom of the market, as illustrated in the property clock in Figure 7.1 below.

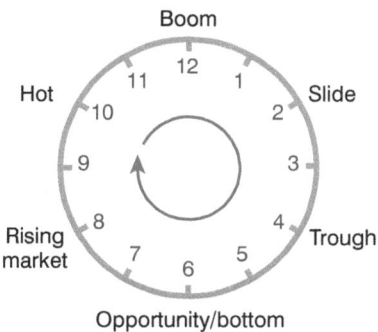

Figure 7.1: The Property Clock

If you do not quite manage to time the market perfectly, do not despair. The real secret to creating wealth from property is twofold: first, you ideally want to keep the property for long enough that it goes through several bursts of growth, allowing you to enjoy strong capital growth over time. Secondly, you want to make sure it is located in an area where you can rent it out easily and continually. That is what good long-term investors do. You will notice, too, that they do not panic when the markets stall, because they know they are playing a long game.

For example, let's say you bought a property in a rising market and then you held it for 20 years. During this time, the market boomed three times. You paid $300,000 for the property and after two decades of ownership, it was worth $800,000, which is an annual average increase of 5 per cent per annum.

Your friend bought a similar property in a similar neighbourhood, only they bought it three years earlier. They only paid

$250,000 for their property and they held it for the same period of time.

The point is, in 20+ years' time, you have both still made a substantial profit. Ideally, you want to buy at the bottom of the market, but time in the market is far more important, because two or three cycles of growth will put you in a great position, regardless.

Point of difference

Once all of the above criteria have been met, the last (but definitely not least) element to tick off your list is a point of difference. This is a unique feature that not only ensures a steady stream of quality renters are lining up to move into your property, but a point of difference also underpins strong long-term capital growth.

When we are helping our clients to build their portfolios, it is very important to us that we assist them to find properties that offer a unique point of difference. So what does this mean exactly?

Think of it this way, if you are looking at a property located in a massive estate and it is just one of 350 to 400 homes that look and feel exactly the same, you do not have much of a point of difference. This can prove problematic if vacancy rates rise, as you have no carrot to dangle in front of potential tenants to entice them to rent your home instead of the cheaper one across the street.

That 'carrot' may come in many forms, such as larger or more bedrooms, a great view, a unique floor plan, a corner block, undercover car parking, a pool or spa, or other additional amenities.

Your property's point of difference could also relate to a strategic location; is it near local employment, close to a beach, bushland or a transport hub? Or if you are in a market where house and land packages are in abundance, but there is one boutique apartment complex in the middle, then that might just be a property with a point of difference.

It is all a matter of supply and demand. In this case, you are offering a chic, one-bedroom apartment to the market and you are only competing against a handful of other potential apartment landlords within your complex. Whereas the 200 or so other property owners in the area are vying for renters' attention with their same four-bedroom houses.

Of course, you would need to do your due diligence and check with local property managers that there is a rental demand for small apartments in the area. If there is, then the property offers a strong point of difference – and you are probably on a winner.

STAGE 3: TRANSITION

Minimising your risk and maximising your profits

THE TRANSITION PHASE is the longest phase you will experience as a property investor, but here is the good news: it is also the most passive.

During the transition phase, you really do not do much of anything other than pay your mortgage, check in with your property manager and watch your property portfolio grow in value!

As we have outlined in the previous chapters, once you have bought all of the investment properties you want to accumulate, you are then going to enter the transition phase, which is where you do not actively buy any more investments.

This is the time period where equity and, eventually, wealth is created.

Whether you have three properties or fifteen properties in your portfolio, this will become your least-active period as a landlord. You will not be saving deposits for future investments; you will not be researching the market to look for buying opportunities. Instead, you will be paying off your mortgages, attending to repairs and maintenance and perhaps renovating parts of your portfolio as and when required.

Meanwhile in the background, capital growth is doing its thing and moving your wealth position in the right direction!

As I have mentioned throughout this book, time in the market is critical to your success. Data from the government land title office and the Real Estate Institute of Australia (REIA) make this point for me.

Between 1975 and 1995, median house prices in our capital cities increased as follows:

- Sydney: $34,300 to $196,750
- Melbourne: $28,700 to $129,000

- Brisbane: $23,700 to $147,000
- Adelaide: $26,150 to $111,500
- Perth: $24,500 to $126,800
- Hobart: $25,850 to $106,750
- Darwin: $87,500[2] up to $165,375
- Tasmania: $33,600 to $155,550

This is made clearer when shown on a graph (see Figure 8.1).

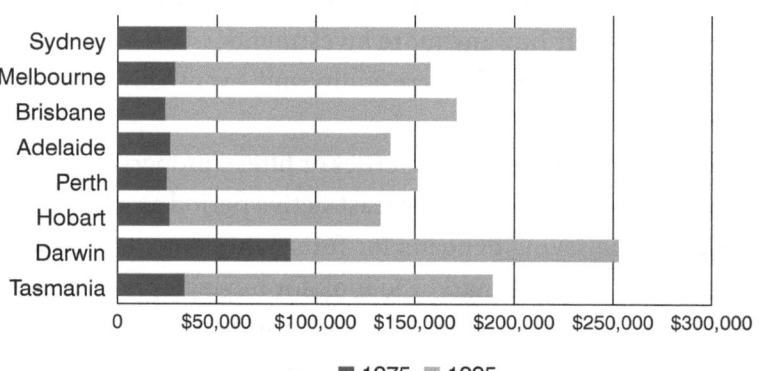

Figure 8.1: Growth in capital city median house prices (1975 to 1995)

Over the space of two decades, property prices increased by up to 550 per cent. Now, they may not have increased in a linear way, growing in value by 5 per cent each year – some years they may have experienced little, no or declining growth, and in others they could have boomed.

But with time in the market you can weather this winding path forward and ultimately enjoy the benefits of long-term capital growth. This is why the transition phase is so important – the longer it is, the more you can potentially benefit from it.

---

2 Macquarie University Department of Economics, Research Paper: Housing Prices in Australia, 1970 to 2003. ^Statistics for Darwin began 1987.

It is clear from this data that if you were an investor in the 1970s and purchased five properties, you would be sitting on an absolute goldmine today. Even if you purchased property in the 1990s, you would still be in possession of a very valuable portfolio today.

You cannot go back in time, so the next best thing is to buy today.

Once you have built a property portfolio, what comes next? The following chapters cover this period by discussing how to manage your properties and minimise your risks while you wait for capital growth to work its magic!

CHAPTER 8

The most costly property investing risks and how to mitigate them

WHEN WE TALK about property investing risks, we are essentially talking about all of the influences, scenarios and events that could derail your financial success.

Some of these are internal risks and you are therefore able to control them to some degree. The rest are external risks, meaning they are well outside of your control – however, that does not mean you cannot prepare for them and mitigate their impacts.

The following property investing risks have the potential to hit you from left, right and centre. When we work with our clients, we arm them with a number of strategies and options to help mitigate or minimise these risks as much as possible. I am going to share some of the most common profit-crunching risks in this chapter, along with some suggestions for overcoming them.

Market risk

The somewhat sad truth of the matter is this: properties do not go up in value all the time. As we discussed in the earlier section on market cycles, they typically go through phases where property prices stagnate, experience a sharp burst of growth and then stagnate again. Occasionally an over-correction occurs, where there is a clear drop in property values.

In other words, property price growth is not one straight, strong line trending up. Every market moves a little differently, but in general you will have a longer period of stagnation, a sudden burst of growth and then it goes around again. As we said, this is called a market cycle.

Remember, it's where you buy within the market cycle that is key, and the other essential part of the process is time in the market. People who hope to buy and quickly sell and make a quick profit are rarely the ones who become wildly successful as investors, because timing the market well can be hard to achieve. Unless you have a crystal ball, timing the market to find the optimal time to buy is challenging, but it is crucial for that strategy to work.

Market risk is present for every investment you will ever make, but overcoming it is all part of your due diligence. When you do your research, you should know what the market is doing, how it has been performing, what the fundamentals are, and what the prospects are like for the future. You can use all of the knowledge to your advantage to plan the best possible approach to your investment.

In saying all of this, however, you have to accept that every property market in Australia moves at various speeds at various times. You cannot always predict what is going to happen – but you can put risk mitigation strategies in place to protect yourself from any fallout.

Mitigate this risk by...

One of the best strategies to mitigate your risk is to keep properties for the longest period possible. The idea is not to buy and quickly sell, or to get despondent if performance is sluggish and sell, or to have a three to four year outlook. Instead, you want to have a plan that allows for 15 to 20 years of property ownership, so it gives you time for your property to go through these growth spurts at least twice. Therefore, eventually, you will enjoy some good capital growth in your property.

Another mitigation strategy we suggest to our clients when putting together their property portfolio is to buy in different locations, because every location in the Australian market has its own cycle. As a result, diversity can be one of your biggest assets as a property investor.

For example, the Gold Coast and Cairns areas in Queensland were badly affected by the GFC and the high Australian dollar because their economies thrive on tourism. A high Australian dollar means fewer international visitors, therefore these local economies suffered for many years after the GFC. During this period however, other markets improved and eventually boomed – most notably, Sydney and Melbourne, which surged during 2013 to 2015.

If you have investment properties in various locations, it is likely to be the case that there is always one location going gangbusters and one that is sluggish.

Liquidity risk

As a property investor, you have to become comfortable with the fact that your money is tied up. Unlike shares, for example, you cannot trade property quickly; finding a buyer takes time, transactions take time to process and each purchase or sale can take up to several months to complete.

This makes property, as an asset class, comparatively difficult to buy and sell. If you buy and sell shares, it is a fairly easy process and you can trade pretty much every minute of the day.

When you buy and sell property, on the other hand, it takes weeks to go through the process of research and due diligence, finance preparation, negotiation on price and processing the transaction.

Furthermore, it is very unlikely that you will make money very quickly in property. Some people make the mistake of thinking property investment is similar to investing in shares, where you can buy one day and see that the investment has grown in value the next day. The property market moves a lot slower than this.

Taxation is also a killer. You pay substantial stamp duty on the way in, and capital gains tax on the way out, which is why few people make big money just by buying and selling properties in the short term.

As a consequence, investors must accept and be comfortable with the fact that property is a long-term investment that will tie up your funds, and you should plan accordingly.

Mitigate this risk by…

…understanding what you are in for as a property investor. If you are in a position where you might need cash very quickly, then investing all of your funds into property does not make sense. Instead, you should create a strategy whereby an amount of money is kept accessible, in a term deposit or a mortgage offset account.

It is important to understand that property is not designed to be an asset class that you trade in and out of frequently; it is for the longer term. When people decide to invest in property, they are in there for the long haul and you should not be looking at buying and selling very quickly, as that generally erodes your profits.

Strategy risk

This is possibly the most common risk that people take every day of the week and it is investing in property without a strategy.

It is quite simple: if you do not plan properly, you set yourself up to fail. I talk to plenty of potential clients each month who call me and say, 'I have a couple of properties, but I am not sure where I am going next and I do not really have a plan.'

This can lead to all sorts of problems, obviously, because when you are investing without clear goals or objectives, it is easy to make unsound decisions based on emotions.

Let's say, for example, that your investment property has not moved in value in three years. You invested in property to create wealth and here you are three years down the track with a property that seems to cost you money rather than move your bank balance forward.

You are fed up, so you decide to sell. You are making this decision because emotions have entered the picture, and because you do not have a clear strategy guiding you forward. If you do decide to sell, you are going to miss out on years or potentially decades of future growth from that investment – and all because you did not have a strategy!

It is essential that you evaluate your properties on the facts and figures and nothing more. When you are buying an investment it is not about property, it is about creating wealth and it is about the numbers.

Furthermore, investing in property on your own without understanding what you are doing is just a recipe for disaster. It is like me trying to repair the toilet in my own home when I knew next to nothing about plumbing, as I discussed earlier in Chapter 5. I had no idea what I was doing, but it did not look complicated on the face of it, so I gave it a go. Then I made a mistake and it ended up costing me a lot more when I had to call in the specialist to fix it anyway.

In property, you are dealing with amounts of money that are much more significant than a routine plumbing job – so why take the risk of trying to do it alone when there is an easier way to create wealth?

Mitigate this risk by...

...speaking to someone who can guide you forward – pronto!

Fortunately, although this is one of the biggest (and potentially most costly) risks you will face as an investor, it is also a relatively easy risk to manage. You simply need to get a team of experts around you, including a good mortgage broker, property adviser, accountant and maybe even a financial planner, to get your strategy back on track.

This will allow you to take stock of where you are now, where you are headed, and where you would like to end up in 5, 10 or 20 years' time.

Interest rate risk

As I mentioned at the start of this chapter, some risks are internal (within your control) and some are external (out of your control). Interest rates are one of the biggest external risks you will deal with as an investor. Many people find this difficult to deal with as interest rates have a huge impact on your property investments.

Having such a huge part of your financial life 'out of your control' can be a scary place to be, especially if you have a low risk profile.

Here is the interesting thing about interest rates, though. The Reserve Bank of Australia (RBA) does not control interest rates; the banks do. The banks will decide, from a commercial point of view, whether they will increase or reduce interest rates.

While they are influenced by what the RBA does, there is no obligation on the banks to pass on any cuts when delivered by the RBA. (Funnily enough, they will quickly pass on a rate increase, you may have noticed!) The banks' priority is to generate profits for their shareholders and they get their profit from borrowers.

This brings me to risk for property investors. Depending on the broader economic environment, interest rates may be low (less than 6 per cent), average (6 to 8 per cent) or high (above 8 per cent). Historically, mortgage interest rates in Australia have usually hovered at around the 7 per cent mark.

If you invest when interest rates are in the lower part of the cycle, you run the risk of assuming that rates will stay this low forever – and that can lead to some very costly situations down the track.

How interest rates could crunch through your cash flow

The impact that an interest rate rise could have on your cash flow really depends on your personal situation. If you are earning $200,000 per annum and you have monthly disposable income of $10,000, then an extra $50 a week on your mortgage repayment is not going to be too difficult to manage. However, if you earn $80,000 a year and you have two kids and your property suddenly becomes $200 cash flow negative per month, then you need a serious plan to make sure you can cope.

Table 8.1 includes a few calculations that demonstrate the impact even a modest interest rate increase can have on your cash flow.

Table 8.1: How increased interest rates can hurt you

Interest rate increase (%)	Monthly increase (annual increase)		
	$300,000 loan	$500,000 loan	$700,000 loan
0.25	$62.50 ($750)	$104 ($1,250)	$146 ($1,750)
0.5	$125 ($1,500)	$208 ($2,500)	$292 ($3,500)
1.0	$250 ($3,000)	$417 ($5,000)	$583 ($7,000)
1.5	$375 ($4,500)	$625 ($7,500)	$875 ($10,500)
2.0	$500 ($6,000)	$833 ($10,000)	$1,167 ($14,000)

Mitigate this risk by...

....Forward planning. Most banks will assess your borrowing power at a default interest rate of around 7 per cent. I feel this is a good risk mitigation strategy in a low interest rate environment. If you are taking out a mortgage when rates are already at this level (7 per cent), then load it by 2 per cent (i.e. increase it to 9 per cent) to make sure your repayments are still affordable.

We do this for our clients so we can ensure they are financially comfortable and they know what their cash flow will be if interest rates increase. Furthermore, we help them come up with a plan to cope financially if interest rates do increase and their property goes from being $50 cash flow positive every week to being $100 cash flow negative.

Generally, this plan involves having financial buffers, which can be in the form of savings, accessible equity or a line of credit. Fixing loans can also be a risk mitigation strategy, but keep in mind it is only a short term 'fix', as your loan will revert to market price at some point.

This form of risk mitigation is absolutely essential because, in my view, it helps nobody if an investor purchases a property that ends up being unaffordable. Part of taking advice when you are investing is finding good advisers who will make sure you are not stretched financially. After all, you are choosing to invest in property to create wealth, and that means using the best and safest method without putting extreme pressure on your finances, leaving you struggling to cope.

Credit risk

Just as you have no control over how much interest the banks are going to charge you, you also have no control over how they will structure their lending policies.

Lenders change their borrowing criteria all the time. As a finance broker, this can be frustrating, I can attest to this! As a borrower, however, it can be very near impossible to navigate, as banks and lenders tend to change the rules of the game every other week.

A typical case to illustrate this risk is the changes that banks made to foreign borrowers between 2014 and 2016. In Melbourne, a number of apartments were released to the market off the plan and they were partially purchased by Chinese investors. Investors signed purchase contracts in 2014 and by the time the properties were completed and due to settle two or three years later, the banks had changed their credit policies.

Suddenly, they decided not to lend as freely to foreigners anymore. Then, they decided not to lend to foreigners at all. There were quite a few buyers who found themselves in serious trouble because they could not settle the properties they had purchased – meaning they were in default of their purchase contract. They faced the possibility of losing their deposit, and worse still, the developer pursuing them for their financial loss.

This is a terrible situation to be in and you may be thinking, 'Well, I'm not a foreign buyer, so this would not impact me.' The reality is that this type of change in lender policy does not only apply to foreigners; banks have got the ability to change the rules whenever they fancy. You just have to consider the fact that investors within Australia felt the brunt of this in 2015 and early 2016, when the Australian Prudential Regulation Authority (APRA) forced lenders to restrict lending to investors.

The problem with this risk is that unless you are independently wealthy, you are likely going to need to borrow from a bank to fund your investments. So how can you overcome this credit risk?

Mitigate this risk by...

...maximising your situation as best as you can. Banks can change the rules on you whenever they choose, by changing the way they calculate borrowing capacity; requiring larger deposits; and even restricting LVRs for certain properties, loan types and borrowers.

To ensure you are always putting your best foot forward (and therefore, you have the best possible chance of being approved for your loan), you need to keep your personal house in order to the best of your ability. To achieve this, you need to do the following:

- Keep a clean credit file
- Pay off your 'bad' debts
- Always pay your bills on time
- Live within your means
- Continue to build your savings/buffer account.

Price appreciation risk

I have said it before and I will say it again: if your property is not poised for growth or experiencing growth, then it is not the right property to have in your portfolio.

Price appreciation is what ultimately drives your wealth as a property investor. Although the cash flow you are achieving within your portfolio may be on track, you run the risk of failing to achieve lasting wealth if your property is not positioned to experience strong capital growth.

We have talked about market cycles and the fact that they do not always move forward in a linear fashion; so how do you determine whether your investment is experiencing capital growth – or is at least poised for growth in the future?

Generally, a market will only be 'suppressed' for a number of years. If the fundamentals are in place – there's a growing population, strong economy and good infrastructure, among other things – then growth should soon be forthcoming.

I have a client who had invested in the suburb of Loganholme in Queensland. He had owned the property for almost 10 years and it had not moved in value, so he was asking if he should sell.

I thought that it was likely that Loganholme might go through a property growth spurt, as 10 years is a long time in any market to go without capital growth. So, my advice was to hold the investment for another one to two years to see what happens next. If no growth is achieved in that time, then he should consider his next move carefully.

He stuck with that property and wouldn't you know it, the growth spurt did happen. His property experienced strong growth and put him in the position of being able to extract equity from the home to leverage into another investment.

Mitigate this risk by...

...continually evaluating your property's performance.

If you buy in the wrong area, or keep your property for too short a timeframe, then you may not get the capital growth you were aiming for and ultimately, you are going to waste your time holding onto it.

By continually evaluating your investments, you can keep an eye on the market to ascertain whether they still deserve a place in your portfolio.

The steps I outlined in the last chapter about buying the 'right' property will help you to avoid buying a low performing, high-risk property. Common sense says you should invest in properties that are going to appeal to tenants, which means investing in homes in areas that have large populations, a growing economy and are in high demand.

Tenancy risk

When you begin investing in property, you may need to change your mindset to become comfortable with the many facets of becoming a landlord.

There are several different risks associated with renting your property out and it is only natural for people to worry about the risks which might eventuate. As a potential landlord, you might be asking yourself the following questions:

- What do we do if our tenants want to move out?
- What if our tenant causes damage to the property?
- What if our tenant does a runner in the middle of the night?
- What if we cannot find a tenant at all and we are stuck paying the mortgage in full every week with no rental income?

These are all real possibilities. There will always be times when one tenant leaves and another does not move in for another week or two, giving you a vacancy period where you need to cover the mortgage in full. This comes with the territory if you are a landlord!

However, these potential risks should not keep you up at night. In fact, as a landlord, these risks should not even rate a mention in your top 10 list of concerns – because there are a number of safe, simple and affordable strategies you can use to minimise their impacts.

Mitigate this risk by...

...Adopting a three-pronged strategy for tenancy success.

- Buy in a good location. There will always be a waiting list

of interest parties lining up to rent your property from you if it's in a good location. Avoid buying in a poor position, such as next to a noisy train line or on a busy main road.
- Use property managers. They are the experts in sourcing and placing quality tenants. Do not attempt to do it yourself just to save a few dollars a week. The hassles of managing your own investment far outweigh the benefits of having this expert on your team!
- Get landlord's insurance. Bad tenants can happen to good people, so make sure you have landlord's insurance in place. This covers you in case a tenant damages the property or sneaks off in the middle of the night without paying their rent.

Procrastination risk

This is an interesting one. Another term I use for procrastinating is dithering; either way, it can be lethal to your wealth!

For most people, when they buy a property they go through phases as outlined in this book. There is the planning phase, the accumulation phase, the transition phase and the drawdown phase – the final phase being the best of all, as this is where you cash in your chips so to speak and enjoy your retirement.

When you are in the planning phase, people tend to go one of two ways: they either rush into purchasing a property, thinking they have to buy now, now, now, and therefore make costly mistakes. Or, and this is a much more common outcome, they realise they need to take their time to do their research, but they get so comfortable with procrastinating that they fail to take any action… at all… for many, many years!

This is such a wasted opportunity as it represents years of lost growth. At some point, you need to be able to say, 'I know what my investing plan is, all of my questions have been answered and now I am ready to buy'. One of the biggest pleasures of my job is when I talk to people in their planning phase and they suddenly 'get it'. There is a look in their eyes that shows me something has clicked into place and they understand how it all works. This is fantastic – and the next step is to actually do things!

Mitigate this risk by...

...making a decision and taking decisive action. If you keep looking and looking and looking, and you never make a decision, you run the risk of taking years before you enter the investment market.

I can almost guarantee you that if you procrastinate, you will have property regrets. I have had clients call me five years after our first meeting and they say, 'I should have bought that property, it has almost doubled in value; I should have bought it when we talked about it years ago!'

Procrastination is a big risk because it is actually an opportunity risk. You are sitting there, wanting to move forward, but if you are not able to make the decision and the commitment, at the end of the day you are going to miss out. Planning is good, but if you are planning for too long, you are moving into procrastination territory and that is not a good place to be.

CHAPTER 9

Is there a *wrong* way to invest?

IF INVESTING IN property were simple and straightforward, everyone in Australia would be doing it. Everyone in Australia would become a landlord. Everyone in Australia would be growing their wealth and ideally getting rich. But that is not the case, and it is because for as many ways as there are to profit from property, there are just as many ways to lose money.

One of the biggest and most common risks of property investing is moving forward without a strategy, as this causes people to make costly financial mistakes. If you do not have a clear idea of why you are investing or what you are aiming to achieve, it can be all too easy to 'jump ship'. It just takes one bad tenant experience, or one whiff that interest rates might be climbing up, to put that fear back into the pit of your stomach. Then boom – your property's on the market and you are suddenly out of the investing game.

I have seen it happen and it really is a shame, as it stops many people from building a strong financial future.

To avoid falling into this trap, I want to use this opportunity to highlight some of the biggest risks in property and how to avoid them. This list does not cover everything that can go wrong – there are actually dozens of 'wrong ways to invest', and I would need an entire book on its own to cover all of them!

But, this will give you an indication of the riskiest strategies and property philosophies that can get new landlords into trouble.

Five poor investment strategies to avoid

Ultimately as an investor, your primary focus should be the fundamentals of a quality investment. I have gone through these in detail throughout this book – I am talking about a central location, growing population and desirable rental area. If you get these fundamentals right, you will minimise your chances of making costly property mistakes.

Let's break down the biggest risks to avoid as a property investor when considering property fundamentals.

Poor investment #1: Investing in low-leverage properties

As an investor, you can choose to invest in all types of properties: apartments, houses, off the plan property, older homes, newer homes, renovated or original condition properties… the list goes on.

One savvy decision that clever investors make to refine their search is to rule out any property that is not new, nearly new or substantially renovated. These are properties that can be highly leveraged in a number of ways, inlcuding:

Depreciation – The building part of a property that is new or nearly new can be depreciated, as can the fixtures and fittings inside the property. The newer the property, the higher the depreciation allowances that you can offset against your taxable income. On a near-new property purchased for $400,000, you may be entitled to up to $10,000 per year (or more) in depreciation deductions. This is a non-cash deduction, so you receive this deduction against your taxable income (and therefore additional income) without having to spend any money!

Lower maintenance costs – Newer properties can cost less to maintain. Unless you are really unlucky, the hot water unit is not going to break down, window screens will not need replacing and electronic garage doors will still be running in good order. Compare this with an older property, which requires more ongoing maintenance as little problems often arise regularly. On top of this, you are faced with the decision of whether to upgrade the kitchen or bathroom to attract a higher rent.

Insurance – With newer and nearly new homes, you are covered by builder's insurance known as the builder's warranty. This means that if in the unlikely event there are structural problems that need fixing, you will not have to pay for them, it will be the builders' responsibility.

A popular view among new investors is that buying older properties to renovate is the ideal strategy, as it allows you to add instant equity. There is nothing wrong with this strategy – in fact it can be a real money-spinner – but it does not always pay off. It only tends to work very well if a number of factors are present, such as:

- You have plenty of time on your hands to dedicate to renovations

- You have extensive experience as a builder or handyman
- You have discretionary funds available to cope with any unexpected extra work you did not anticipate when planning the renovation. You never know what defect will surface!
- You can command a better yield with a renovated property than a new property. Even though your renovation work can be depreciated, it will not be as high as the depreciation deduction on a new property, so you may need more rent to compensate. (See scenario below.)

Again, this all comes back to your strategy. If a renovation strategy makes the most sense for you and your situation, then you could go down this path. Personally, I prefer passive properties that I do not need to invest my time into, so I look at property as a financial product and therefore go for new investments on a 'set and forget' basis.

Depreciation in action

Let's look at an example to highlight how a low-leverage property can impact your investments, with an explanation of the difference depreciation can make to your cash flow.

Table 9.1 on the next page shows the profit and loss account and cash flow of a new 'moderately priced' property at $440,000.

Table 9.1: Profit and loss cash flow: $440,000 property (with depreciation)

Profit and loss account		Price	Year 1
Rent			$430
Income	Occupancy ratio	95%	$21,242
Interest	Interest	Loan	
	4.7%	90%	
	Loan amount	$396,000	($18,612)
Management fees		8.8%	($1,869)
Rates		3%	($2,500)
Other		3%	($2,000)
Cash flow before the effect of taxation			($3,739)
Depreciation			($10,840)
Total tax loss			($14,579)
Tax refund	Marginal rate	39%	$5,686
Cash flow before the effect of taxation			($3,739)
Add tax refund			$5,686
Cash flow	Per annum		$1,947
	Per week		$37

As you can see, the property shows a tax loss in year 1 of $14,579, of which $10,840 is due to depreciation. This allows the investor – we have assumed the investor earns between $100,000 and $180,000 per annum – to claim back $5,686 at a tax rate of 39 per cent (which is 37 per cent tax rate plus 2 per cent Medicare Levy).

Before taking into account taxation, this property is cash flow negative by $3,739 per annum or $72 per week. But thanks to depreciation, the cash flow becomes positive by $1,947 per annum or $37 a week.

This is a perfect example of how a negatively geared property with a tax loss can actually be cash flow positive. The key to success here is to maximise depreciation.

From this example, you can easily see that if you buy an old property with no depreciation, your cash flow is going to be a lot worse, as demonstrated in Table 9.2 below.

Table 9.2: Profit and loss cash flow: $440,000 property (no depreciation)

Profit and loss account		Price	Year 1
Rent			$430
Income	Occupancy ratio	95%	$21,242
Interest	Interest 4.7%	Loan 90%	
	Loan amount	$396,000	($18,612)
Management fees		8.8%	($1,869)
Rates		3%	($2,500)
Other		3%	($2,000)
Cash flow before the effect of taxation			($3,739)
Depreciation			$0
Total tax loss			($3,739)
Tax refund	Marginal rate	39%	$1,458
Cash flow before the effect of taxation			($3,739)
Add tax refund			$1,458
Cash flow	Per annum		($2,281)
	Per week		($44)

Without depreciation, this property is now cash flow negative by $2,281 per annum or $44 a week, as we are not able to use depreciation as leverage.

How much higher does the rent need to be in an older property to compensate for the lack of depreciation? The answer is a lot higher. You would need the rent to be more than 35 per cent of the current market return, reaching a staggering $584 a week in order to achieve the same financial result as obtained with depreciation!

Table 9.3: Achieving the same return without depreciation

Profit and loss account		Price	Year 1
Rent			$584
Income	Occupancy ratio	95%	$28,842
Interest	Interest 4.7%	Loan 90%	
	Loan amount	$396,000	($18,612)
Management fees		8.8%	($2,538)
Rates		3%	($2,500)
Other		3%	($2,000)
Cash flow before the effect of taxation			$3,192
Depreciation			$0
Total profit before tax			$3,192
Tax paid	Marginal rate	39%	($1,245)
Cash flow before the effect of taxation			$3,192
Less tax paid			($1,245)
Cash flow	Per annum		$1,947
	Per week		$37

You will also notice that in the scenario shown in Table 9.3, the property will have a taxable profit and therefore income tax will be payable. Of course, if there is a renovation involved there will be some small depreciation you can claim, but it is nowhere near enough to turn the numbers around in a substantial way.

My recommendation is always purchase a new or newer property when given the opportunity, rather than an older home. Even with renovations factored in, the numbers give you a clear answer as to which investment is better for your bottom line.

Poor investment #2: Over-committing to properties you cannot afford

Another common risk of property investing is over-committing to your portfolio. You can then end up in a situation where your properties are not making you rich, but instead are draining your finances every week and you risk ending up in the poor house.

It can be difficult to see this risk when you are the one in the middle of a 'less than ideal' property situation.

For example, I have a client who came to me stating that she had bought an old house worth $900,000 in a suburb of Brisbane. It was close to the CBD and had a long list of tenants lining up to move in, so it ticked those boxes.

However, she had purchased it with a 90 per cent loan, which meant she had borrowed $810,000 + LMI. Her mortgage was therefore very high. She received $650 rent per week, which is a fairly low yield for the price she paid – it certainly falls well short of my 'rule of one thousand'.

However, she felt that because her existing property was in a sought-after location, close to the CBD, she was assured capital growth. As a result, she felt that she had to accept that the property had a negative cash flow as the cost of doing business.

She came to me because she wanted to buy a second property, a cheaper one this time! But I had some concerns, as there were a number of red flags.

Red flag: She did not know her cash flow

At the time we spoke, she was paying just over 4 per cent on an interest-only loan for her Brisbane investment. She said that she could manage the cash flow, although she did not know how much it was exactly, but she expected a tax refund at the end of the year to help her cover the property costs. We did the calculations for her and it turned out that even with tax deductions and depreciation factored in, the cash flow was negative by about $200 per week. That is a $10,000 cash shortfall every single year.

Red flag: She had no depreciation

Because the property was older and not renovated, her tax refund was quite low, as there was virtually no depreciation to claim. She had never been educated about the power of depreciation and was missing out on this huge cash flow benefit.

Red flag: She had no plan in place to deal with interest rate rises

At the time of purchasing the property, this investor's mortgage was manageable as she was paying interest of around 4 per cent. But she failed to take into consideration how much her mortgage would cost her if interest rates were to increase. I modelled what would happen if interest rates went up to 7 per cent. She was horrified when I told her that her cash flow would then be negative at an amount of over $500 per week! That is more than $25,000 in losses every single year. She would want to be very sure that her capital growth projections more than made up for this loss!

Needless to say, she put a pause on her next investment while she considered what to do next. Her situation was not yet dire, but it could have become very seriously stressful and unmanageable.

My recommendation is that it is essential for every investor to forward-plan the future of their portfolio to avoid over-committing and ending up in financial hot water. Do not just look at what you can afford today; plan ahead for interest rate increases. You could consider changing your loan to pay the interest only rather principal and interest. This will reduce your repayments to ensure you can afford your properties long term.

Poor investment #3: Digging yourself into a financial hole

The goal of property investing is to ultimately grow your wealth and make you rich, but it is surprising how many people achieve the absolute opposite outcome to this.

For some, real estate leads to a path of financial ruin. It is usually because they are not educated about investing the right way, so they dig themselves into a financial hole that is almost impossible to get out of.

This was a huge problem following the GFC, when many people ended up in a negative equity situation. Investors bought property for say $500,000 and the value of their property dropped to say $440,000. They had a mortgage for $450,000, so they actually owed more on their asset than what it was worth. As it turned out, property values in Australia recovered quickly to pre-GFC levels 18 months later in all well-located areas, so the people affected were only those people who needed to sell immediately.

However, this is a terribly stressful position to find yourself in. I was once contacted by someone who was very upset, as he found himself struggling with a portfolio of four properties he had bought during the mining boom. Unfortunately, all of the properties he had bought were located in mining towns. He knew about the golden rule of diversification, but he thought that buying in Karratha, Kalgoorlie, Moranbah and Cessnock was diversified enough.

When the mining boom ended, he bitterly regretted not listening to people around him. He had put all of his eggs in one basket by investing solely in mining towns and it had not paid off for him. He wanted advice on what to do next.

Sometimes, property decisions are made that are poorly thought out or not well planned and it may be the case that there is no turning back and no way to rectify the situation – other than selling the property. This could even mean selling at a huge loss.

Unfortunately for this client, we had to go down this path. Luckily, his Cessnock property had some equity in it and by chipping in $25,000 from his savings, he was able to sell two of his low-performing properties.

He was still stuck with another two properties in mining towns, but at least by selling two, his risk was spread over two properties and not four. As the post mining boom saw interest rates drop to record lows, he was able to afford the lower cash flow.

His strategy shifted to focus on debt repayment. His plan was to save as much as he could to pay the loans down, while interest rates were low. This may not make him rich, but it would allow him to avoid losing everything – and hopefully put him in a position where he could invest again in the future.

My recommendation is that making a property loss is no one's idea of a good time! It can be challenging to get your head around, but sometimes it is the only way forward. Working with a property adviser can help you to review your situation objectively and without emotion, so you can see all of the options available to you and move forward.

Poor investment #4: Joint partnerships

Those in the property industry often promote joint partnerships as a more affordable and faster way to build your property portfolio. Investing with a sibling or a friend could be a way of getting into a property faster: you can split the deposit, split the costs and split the risks. For these reasons, I can understand why it is quite common for investors who have reached their borrowing limits to look for ways to overcome this limitation by embarking on a joint venture.

I should point out that I am excluding from this discussion husband and wife or long-term de facto couples, as they are considered a 'household' from a relationship and financial point of view. What I am talking about is when two separate people – such as friends, siblings, colleagues or business partners – who have come together to purchase an investment.

Although I have no problem with property partnerships in general, this arrangement needs to be very well thought through.

For example, an investor from Townsville in Queensland came to me and told me that he was a mining supervisor and owned five properties. Some of these were purchased with his long-term girlfriend and some were bought as joint ventures with some of his miner friends.

He now wanted to buy property number six on his own. Despite his high salary, I could not obtain another loan for him and he was really surprised.

The reason for this is that when you apply for a loan together with someone else, you are 'jointly and severally liable' for the debt. In other words, both borrowers are responsible for 100 per cent of the debt. From the bank's point of view, this ensures that in the event one defaults, the other is responsible for it.

Let's say you and your brother invest in a property worth $400,000. You jointly obtain a loan of $360,000.

You may consider your financial responsibility to be $180,000 – but in the bank's view, it is far more than that. They will assess you as being responsible for the full $360,000 they have lent you, as they want to be sure that you can manage the loan if your investment partner cannot.

In the case of my client in Townsville, when he was applying for loan number six, the lenders wanted the investor to be sure he could service all of his existing loans as if he were the only borrower. As a result, he could not go ahead with another property.

The only way he could obtain a loan was to borrow in partnership with someone else again. I warned him that over time, he would have to find more and more partners for his applications as the servicing hurdle became higher and higher. As a result, his portfolio building strategy had to be completely reworked.

You may choose to go down the joint-venture path once at the beginning of your journey, simply to get your foot in the market. But keep in mind that once you start investing in a partnership with a friend or family member, you may be condemned to do this for every future loan.

The other substantial risk you have with this strategy is that you can be friends today and foes tomorrow. Your situation could change for a number of reasons and you might want out of the deal, but your joint venture partner does not want to sell – what happens then?

My recommendation is that joint ventures come with a number of risks and complexities, so much so that I could fill an entire chapter! But for now I will simply say that in my view, you should think twice before going down this route.

Poor investment #5: Commercial real estate

When devising a property investing strategy, people often ask me why the focus is generally on residential real estate and not commercial property, especially considering that the transaction is stacked in the landlord's favour in commercial real estate.

For those who do not know, with a commercial property lease the yields are usually far higher than residential and the tenant usually pays the outgoings. Expenses such as council rates and water usage become the responsibility of the tenant, not the landlord – you may even be able to structure property upgrades and renovations into the lease!

With so many on-paper benefits, why do more people not invest in commercial property and why do I consider it to be a risky move?

There is nothing wrong with investing in commercial and industrial real estate per se – except that the risks are much higher and the capital gains are usually much lower.

For example, for most investors, the prospect of having their property without a tenant for six months to a year is just not affordable, yet in commercial real estate, it is not uncommon to have these gaps between tenants.

A pertinent example is my own! In the first half of 2016, I moved our business into new premises as a tenant. The office we moved into had been empty for seven months. It is well located in a busy suburb of Sydney, near a train station and close to other commercial businesses – and yet it still took that long to rent out.

This lack of income can be very stressful if you have a mortgage to pay, which is why commercial property investment is generally suited to those who have little debt secured by the property. Therefore, the need for regular cash inflow is not as critical as it is for a salaried investor who borrows 80 per cent.

My recommendation is that if you have a huge deposit to play with to secure a low LVR, and you have plenty of buffer saved for a rainy day, then commercial real estate may make sense to add to your portfolio. But generally speaking, it is a lot more stressful for your finances!

STAGE 4: DRAWDOWN

Creating your ultimate wealth

As YOU KNOW by now, the property investing philosophy that I follow is based on four key phases: planning, accumulation, transition and drawdown. One phase cannot exist without the other if you want to successfully create wealth as a real estate investor.

You cannot start buying properties without a plan, as you will have no idea what to buy. In the same way, you cannot drawdown on your property portfolio and live on your investment income only three years after you have bought the properties. Well, you could if you used some very complex and high-stakes strategies such as developing, but that is a topic to be covered in a whole new book!

This final phase of your property investing journey is obviously the most enjoyable, because when you go into the drawdown phase, you are actually cashing in your wealth.

The aim of the game is that you will have created financial growth in abundance, so you can go happily ever after into retirement. This may involve you deciding to sell some properties, or sell all of your properties to release the gains and make some serious money out of your investments.

At Multifocus Properties & Finance, we work with our clients to teach them a number of exit strategies that can maximise the amount of money they make at this end stage of the game. In the following pages, I am going to explain some of the more common methods you can use to realise your wealth.

Be aware that every person will need to use a different strategy to unlock their wealth. Your final outcome depends on a number of factors including your risk profile, your investing budget, the actual properties in your portfolio and the capital growth you have achieved over the years.

There are a number of complex factors that come into play, including tax strategy and superannuation, so it is always advisable to work with your team – your accountant, financial planner and property adviser – when planning your exit from the workforce.

However, to inspire you about what may be possible in your future, let's look at the fantastic financial results that can be achieved when you use property to fuel your retirement plan.

CHAPTER 10
Transition to wealth and retirement

WHEN YOU ARE planning to invest in property, you must create time for each of the four phases of wealth creation – planning, accumulation, transition and drawdown – to play out.

In the scenarios that we have used throughout this book, we have assumed that you need $2 million in property assets in order to make $100,000 in passive income in retirement. Now I am talking about the really exciting part of the property investing process, as this is when your wealth is realised!

As an investor, after you have acquired property over a number of years, you will transition to wealth and enter the drawdown phase. There are a number of things you have to consider before you start to access your property returns, such as:

- Your current age and planned retirement age
- Your desired lifestyle in retirement
- The performance of your portfolio.

Your planned retirement age

Your ideal retirement age will have been determined many years earlier. This would largely depend on when you started investing.

If you started out as an investor in your twenties then you could be leaving your day job in your forties. If you bought your first rental property at the age of 45, you will have planned for a shorter investment lifecycle.

As you approach your target retirement age, you will need to re-assess whether this is still achievable and plan to transition into retirement.

Your desired lifestyle in retirement

The exact date you stop working will be influenced by your desired lifestyle in retirement. Do you plan to travel? A little, or a lot? Do you plan to buy a boat? Are you going to get involved in expensive hobbies, such as golf? Would you like to have a holiday home to retreat to (and pay for the maintenance on?) The lifestyle you ideally want to live in retirement will come with a price-tag, which is paid for by your target retirement income.

The performance of your portfolio

With the right planning and due diligence, you will ideally have set yourself up with a property portfolio that has delivered strong long-term growth. But every investor does face the risk of not achieving the goal they set out to accomplish – with lower portfolio growth meaning they may live off $70,000 in retirement instead of $100,000. There are a number of risk mitigation strategies you can use to combat this risk which I discuss below.

Making extra mortgage repayments during transition

For many investors, the ideal investing strategy involves owning a property portfolio that they never sell – ever. Instead, they plan to own their properties and live off the rental income in retirement, until one day they pass on their investments to their loved ones.

To achieve this, you will need to be an active investor over the years. If you have a 30-year investment timeline, the rental income generated over the years may be sufficient to pay off your mortgages entirely. However, being proactive and making extra repayments over time can have an incredible impact on your property goals.

If, during the transition phase, you can start repaying your loans bit-by-bit, you will ensure that by contributing a little extra here and there, you will be closer to owning your properties outright at retirement age. Table 10.1 below shows the impact that even small extra repayments can make.

Table 10.1: The overall impact of extra monthly loan repayments

Loan amount at 5% interest rate	Extra repayment per month*	Total interest savings	Loan repaid
$300,000	$100	$39,937	3 years 8 months earlier
$300,000	$200	$69,210	6 years 5 months earlier
$500,000	$100	$39,937	2 years 4 months earlier
$500,000	$200	$77,470	4 years 2 months earlier
$700,000	$100	$43,860	1 years 8 months earlier
$700,000	$200	$81,693	3 years 2 months earlier

Source: InfoChoice.com.au (http://www.infochoice.com.au/calculators/extra-loan-repayments-calculator/). Assumes extra payments are made from the first mortgage repayment.

These extra repayments can make a huge impact but of course, they do add up over time. If you have five properties in your portfolio and you are paying an additional $200 on the mortgage every month for each one, you will need to find an additional $1,000 per month or $12,000 per year in after-tax dollars.

Consider it this way, when you are doing this you are no longer actively buying properties because you are in the transition phase waiting for them to appreciate in value. This means you no longer need to save your funds towards property deposits, stamp duty and legal fees. You may also have fewer financial commitments associated with bringing up a family – no more school fees to pay, for example. And you may also have been lucky enough to receive an inheritance. Any extra cash could go towards paying down property loans at this stage in the investment process.

If you can afford to make extra mortgage repayments this can be a powerful way to grow your equity. Importantly, it will mean that hopefully by the time you get to retirement age, you will be enjoying a strong cash flow from your portfolio that will deliver the numbers you want as an income stream during your retirement.

Transitioning to wealth

There are a number of strategies you can use to access the wealth you have created in your property portfolio. By working with a financial planner and a property adviser, you can gain a very clear, customised understanding of how your future wealth could eventuate.

To give you some inspiration and understanding of how the transition and drawdown stage can work in real life, I am going to walk you through a number of different scenarios.

Remember, the wonderful thing about this process is that the examples I am about to give you represent everyday, ordinary people who have not done anything 'special' to generate their property wealth. They have simply plotted a course and followed it – and in retirement, they have financial security and peace of mind as a reward for their many years of patience and persistence.

Transition strategy 1: Pay loans down and live off rental income

If you are fortunate enough to reach retirement with a fully paid property portfolio, you will be in a position to enjoy a double whammy in retirement: rental income and capital growth.

By paying all of your investment loans back, by the time you retire you will not have to sell anything, as your rental income stream will be coming in with no mortgage repayments eating into the income. You will still need to pay for the property's upkeep and maintenance and there will be bills to cover such as council rates and property management fees, but the majority of your rental income – around 70 per cent or more – will be yours to enjoy, free and clear each month.

Better yet, you are still exposed to capital growth in your portfolio as you have not sold any assets. At some point, you may start selling your properties for a number of reasons. For example, they are getting older and costing you more to maintain; you no longer want the responsibility of owning properties; or you want all of your funds to be liquid. The best thing about this outcome is that you have bought yourself options so you can slowly, at your leisure, start selling your properties without any financial pressure.

Example

Let's say you start investing in property in your twenties, like our example couple, Jane and Jeremy.

Jane and Jeremy buy five investment properties over a period of 10 years. By the time they are 65 and 70 years of age, these properties are fully paid off. In retirement, Jane and Jeremy own a portfolio similar to that shown in Table 10.2 below (remember, all figures are estimated in today's dollars, not accounting for inflation):

Table 10.2: Jane and Jeremy's property portfolio

Properties	Rental income/week
Property 1 value: $400,000	$400
Property 2 value: $450,000	$450
Property 3 value: $500,000	$500
Property 4 value: $550,000	$550
Property 5 value: $600,000	$600
Total value: $2,500,000	Total income: $2,500

Jane and Jeremy enjoy a rental income of $130,000 per year in retirement, assuming there are no vacancies.

If we subtract 10 per cent to allow for vacancy periods and another 20 per cent to allow for the costs of owning and maintaining the property (for council rates, etc.), they are left with $91,000 each year in rental income to fund their lifestyle.

One thing to keep in mind is that if you reach retirement age and all of your properties are producing a positive income with no mortgages to offset them, then you will need to pay income tax. Depending on the tax rates of the day, this could see you handing over a decent chunk of your rental income to the taxman.

In our example with Jane and Jeremy, a rental income (after expenses) of $91,000 would attract taxes of around $20,000. Be sure to speak to your accountant to talk about strategies available to you to minimise your tax.

Transition strategy 2: Selling your entire portfolio

The second transition strategy for investors to use is to sell off their entire portfolio. This means that when you reach retirement age, you sell off all of your investments, put your cash profits in the bank and live off the interest of your term deposits for the rest of your life.

This is a great option for those who wish to retire with no more responsibilities. But here is a key consideration that many people fail to factor in: if you want $2 million left in the bank for retirement, you will need to create a portfolio worth $2.5 to $3 million in today's money.

This is because once you sell your property and you make a capital gain, the taxman will come along and take his share. You will need to factor this into your calculations to ensure that you end up with $2 million in the bank, to deliver your $100,000 annual income.

Another point I would like to mention here is that your $2 million goal may be partly funded from your superannuation or other investments. Whatever the make-up, the goal in this scenario is to end up with $2 million cash for retirement.

Under this strategy when you get to your retirement age, you will then go into what we call the drawdown phase, which is where you monetise the equity you have accumulated in your portfolio by selling your property assets.

Example

Let's say you start investing in property in your forties and early fifties, like our example couple, Diane and Derek.

Diane and Derek buy seven investment properties over a period of 15 years. By the time they are 65 and 70 years of age, these properties are almost entirely paid off. In retirement, Diane and Derek own a portfolio similar to that shown in Table 10.3 (remember, all figures are estimated in today's dollars, not accounting for inflation).

Table 10.3: Diane and Derek's property portfolio

Properties	Rent
Property 1 value: $300,000	$300
Property 2 value: $350,000	$350
Property 3 value: $400,000	$400
Property 4 value: $450,000	$450
Property 5 value: $500,000	$500
Property 6 value: $550,000	$550
Property 7 value: $600,000	$600
Total value: $3,150,000	Total income: $3,150

In this scenario, Diane and Derek sell their portfolio and spend around $950,000 in selling costs, paying out remaining mortgages and capital gains tax. This leaves them with around $2,200,000 in cash proceeds.

Under this strategy, Diane and Derek put these proceeds from their property sales in the bank and they enjoy a safe, secure and consistent income every single month until the day they die.

However, just as with our first strategy, where Jane and Jeremy had to pay the taxman on their income, Diane and Derek will also need to pay tax.

If they are earning bank interest of 5 per cent, their income in retirement is $110,000. In today's money (and under our current tax regime), they would be required to pay tax of around $30,000 on that interest income. Again, this would need to be factored in and considered alongside your accountant's advice.

Transition strategy 3: Selling part of your portfolio

In a sense, this is a hybrid strategy of the two previously outlined strategies. It involves selling some properties and holding onto the rest. As a result, this final strategy is also the most flexible, as it allows for the greatest level of evolution and pivoting as your portfolio develops.

This is all about choosing your next path when you reach retirement age. You may decide to sell enough properties to repay your outstanding mortgages and then enjoy the income stream on the rest of your portfolio.

You don't have to sell them all at the same time. Perhaps you have an older property that is more maintenance-intensive? That could go first. Then you might sell off further properties in the early years of your retirement, holding them for as long as possible to benefit from ongoing capital gain.

The choice is yours and can depend on many factors, including growth in your portfolio, changes to your financial situation over time and your desired lifestyle in retirement. This is why this strategy is so great – it is very flexible and allows you to adapt your retirement strategy with your changing lifestyle.

The number of properties you sell will depend on the value of those properties, the cash flow you get and the amount of debt you still have to pay.

Example

Let's say you start investing in property in your thirties or forties, like our example couple, Rachel and Rick.

Rachel and Rick buy eight investment properties over a period of 15 years. By the time they are 65 and 70 years of age, these properties are partially paid off. In retirement, Rachel and Rick own a portfolio similar to that shown in Table 10.4 (remember, all figures are estimated in today's dollars, not accounting for inflation).

Table 10.4: Rachel and Rick's property portfolio

Properties	Mortgage	Equity	Rent
Property 1 value: $300,000	$50,000	$250,000	$300
Property 2 value: $350,000	$100,000	$250,000	$350
Property 3 value: $400,000	$120,000	$280,000	$400
Property 4 value: $450,000	$130,000	$320,000	$450
Property 5 value: $500,000	$150,000	$350,000	$500
Property 6 value: $550,000	$200,000	$350,000	$550
Property 7 value: $600,000	$250,000	$350,000	$600
Property 8 value: $650,000	$300,000	$350,000	$650
Total value: $3,800,000	Total mortgage: $1,300,000	Total income: $2,500,000	Total income: $3,800

In this scenario, Rachel and Rick have $1.3 million worth of mortgages still owing, against a portfolio worth almost $4 million. They are receiving weekly rent of $3,800 – meaning their portfolio is very cash flow positive.

In fact, their mortgage repayments on $1.3m are around $2,000 per week, so they presently enjoy a positive cash flow of $1,800 each week. After other ownership expenses of $800 per week, they are left with $1,000 cash flow. To date, they have been reinvesting this excess back into their excess mortgages to accelerate pay down.

At this point, Rachel and Rick have the following options:

- Stay as they are, but use the $1,000 positive cash flow each week to live off, alongside other retirement income such a pension from their superannuation.
- Sell two or three properties so they can pay off their outstanding mortgages and live off the rental income.
- Sell all of their properties, pay off their outstanding mortgages and put their final profits into the bank, so they can live off the interest.

Each of these options has benefits and drawbacks, including different tax advantages and disadvantages. There is no 'right' or 'wrong' way to move forward here – just plenty of options, all of which give you greater choice and more financial freedom in retirement.

Outrunning the risks of real estate-funded retirement

When you are planning to retire, it can seem quite hard to predict the future growth of your portfolio and your income requirements; it is a little like the government preparing the federal budget! You are trying to foresee how much your properties will increase in value, how much your interest rates are going to be, how well the market is going to perform and how much money you will ultimately need in retirement.

This can be a hard prediction to get right. For instance, in planning your retirement you may be on track towards achieving the goal that you want – however for whatever reason, instead of getting the $100,000 income that you want, you get $70,000.

This is why I suggest that you should always buy a couple more properties than you need to achieve your goals. This way you have a backup, so to speak.

If everything goes according to plan, then that is fine – you will simply exceed your target and be in a position to retire earlier. But if there are any rough patches on your investment journey, such as lower than expected growth or higher than expected interest rates, you have additional assets to help make up for any shortfall. This is one form of risk mitigation to consider when putting your retirement plan together. As discussed throughout this book, there are many other risk minimisation tactics you can use to make sure that your properties are growing at the right pace, such as buying blue-chip property stock in the right location.

There is always an element of chance involved, in the sense

that if you could predict the capital growth for each suburb for the next 20 years, then everybody would be rich! There are no crystal balls here, which is why your research must be impeccable. That way, you can be confident that you are buying in a good area with strong fundamentals for future growth. You are not guaranteed success by doing so, but you are certainly putting yourself and your investments at the front of the pack.

CHAPTER 11
Educate and consolidate

AS INVESTING IS quite a simple concept in principle, people often get started thinking that buying rental properties and becoming a landlord is easy. In a sense, they are onto something: to be successful as a property investor, you do not need to know any 'secret recipe' or uncover any complicated strategies. You simply need to invest with clear focus, strategy and planning.

But that does not mean property investing is easy. There are many different parts of the process, from research and negotiation, to buying, property management and tax, and each of these moving parts must work together in a certain way to produce a profitable outcome.

This is why so many first-time investors end up making costly mistakes; because they have not had the education and support to do things the right way from the very beginning.

In this chapter, as I talk about education and consolidation of everything I have discussed so far, I want you to keep in mind that every person in life has a particular speciality. In working to complete a task, it is my view that we should all stick to what we know and leverage other people's skills for those parts of the job we are not familiar with.

My area of expertise is property investing, finance, loans and wealth creation. Throughout this book I have shared with you a number of strategies and steps that my clients use to set themselves up for a successful property investing experience.

The main purpose behind these strategies is to help you make informed decisions. Because here is the truth of the matter: if you are just starting out as an investor and you do not have expert support and guidance, you are going to make a bunch of mistakes.

The majority of investors learn good investment strategies through a process of trial and error – I can vouch for the fact that this is a costly way to go about things! I also think this approach is a waste of time and money, as it is completely avoidable. There are people who have already been on that journey and learnt the hard way and you can benefit from their knowledge and experience.

There are significant benefits for investors who seek the help of a mentor or advocate, as they can help you at every stage of the process, including:

- Making the most appropriate investment decisions
- Creating a solid investment strategy
- Sourcing your next investment property
- Planning your retirement.

Most importantly, when you work with a mentor, you can avoid making what I call 'beginners' mistakes'.

We can learn from the story of evolution. In prehistoric times, humans had to learn how to survive in a harsh environment and they often made terrible mistakes in the process. Yet over time, they learned from their mistakes.

In other words, we are successful when we can learn from our mis-steps and ensure we do not make them again. It is like I always say to my employees: I do not mind if you make a mistake, but do not make it twice.

The profit-risk of investing without professional support

There are many risks in investing without professional support and some of them can be financially devastating. When you are investing with little or no prior knowledge or experience, you are pretty much going into things blind, which means you are more likely to trip and fall at every obstacle. Unfortunately, this is a very common scenario. But rather than tell you about these risks, I want to share with you an example.

Many years ago I knew of a couple who lived in Perth and who had invested in a portfolio of five properties. This couple were getting nowhere with these investments and they wanted to know what I could do to help.

They had started buying in very small regional towns in New South Wales, buying properties for $170,000 and achieving $170 rent per week. Initially, they thought these properties were a fantastic investment – until they realised that there was no capital growth in them and their investments were actually going nowhere. These little towns where they had invested only had 2,000 to 3,000 residents and what they discovered is that once there was a vacancy, it was very hard to find another tenant.

At any given time, out of the five properties they owned, two were generally vacant, because there was not enough of a rental population to keep their properties tenanted all year-round.

I identified two immediate and very big risks within their property portfolio. They had five good quality properties, however they were not cash flow positive because they could not find a tenant, and they had no capital growth for the simple reason that they bought in the wrong location.

Unable to see what was wrong with their strategy, they found themselves in significant trouble.

The plan we came up with basically required them to scratch what they had accumulated and start from the beginning again. This meant they had to sell most of those properties. Eventually, the couple were so dejected by what had happened they never invested again.

Learning through trial and error

I have had my own bad experiences when investing without proper advice. I started investing after talking to someone whose property investments were doing okay and he seemed to know what he was doing. After meeting him and seeing his 'success', I figured I could build and manage an investment portfolio myself. After all, I was in the corporate world and it was all about numbers; what could go wrong?

I had a strategy, though I know now that it was not a very good one. I wanted to create a property portfolio and decided to invest in a wide range of property types. I wanted to try a bit of everything. As I told you in the opening chapter, I bought a house and land package, a retirement home and an apartment. I also bought an existing property that was a few years old, a newish-townhouse, a detached house and a property near a university in a capital city. I invested in a bit of everything, hoping to learn how property investment works along the way. Now in hindsight, I do not think this was a good strategy at all. I should have done more research and developed an understanding of what was going to work for me.

But as it turns out these properties have all been a great source of experience, giving me many lessons that I can pass on to my clients now. By learning through experience and consolidating my knowledge, I have been able to guide other investors forward to enjoy more success sooner from their portfolios than I personally experienced.

I have told you about one of the great successes in my portfolio, the property I bought in St Lucia, near the University of Queensland in Brisbane. You will remember that it is a townhouse and although it is not officially student accommodation, it now has three students living in it. It is doing very well because, being in the centre of Brisbane, it has capital growth. Furthermore, with three students renting it, I am enjoying a fantastic yield.

Much less successful is my retirement unit. It was cheap at the time of purchase and I thought, 'I am not taking much risk here', so I bought it; it was priced under $100,000 so it really felt like a no-lose situation.

If I wanted to sell it today, I could not sell it for any more money than I bought it for 10 years ago. The cash flow for this property was great in the beginning and it is still very cash flow positive, but there is no capital growth in it. Because the cash flow is so strong, I have decided to keep it in my portfolio but I know that it will never surge in growth and if I could go back in time, I would not purchase it.

Another lesson I learned from experience is the importance of researching every single aspect of a deal, down the quality of the builder involved in constructing the property. I am not just talking about new properties, either. I once bought a home in

Townsville in far north Queensland that was about seven years old when I bought it.

At the time I did not know who built it and I really did not give it much thought. Yet that was another valuable lesson for me. When you are buying an existing property, you really need to make sure you know who the builder was because with that knowledge you can get an idea of the quality of the house.

It turned out that there were a number of issues with the building that cost me around $10,000 to fix. For instance, the roof pitch was not steep enough which created problems with water seeping into the house. When I was getting the roof fixed, the repairer told me that the property had been built by a particular builder who had a reputation for dodgy work. That was a light bulb moment for me; no wonder I was having problems with it! Nonetheless, that property in Townsville is now doing very well and it has experienced solid capital growth, while delivering strong cash flow.

After that experience, I realised I would always need to know who the builders are. To do that, I would need to buy houses that are near-new, so that if there is any trouble I know who built the property and I can contact them to rectify the work. If you buy older stock, you may never know who the builder was and you do not know what problems might arise.

The value of a good investment strategy

I know I have gone on about this at length throughout this book, but it is because a good investment strategy is so integral to your success! Investing without a clear strategy to guide you forward is just plain dangerous. You can never know exactly how your properties will perform but you can educate and inform yourself so you can increase the likelihood of a positive outcome.

Above all, when you are buying investment properties, it is essential that you ask yourself the following three questions:

1. Is the property in the right location?
2. Am I buying at the right time?
3. Is this the right type of property for this market?

These are the types of questions that will help you keep your investment strategy on track, as your answers will guide your purchase decisions.

Your strategy is typically tailored around your current financial situation. By way of example, I will use a very common profile that we see in our clients: they are a couple with one or two kids and they own their home with a partly-paid mortgage remaining.

The kids are almost in their teens and the couple is much more comfortable financially than they were when they were just starting their family. These clients are often aged in their forties, and they have started thinking about what they are going to do when they retire. Looking at their finances, they realise their superannuation fund is inadequate.

Thinking about what they can do to support their superannuation, they consider property investment. If you are in this type of situation, real estate can be a pretty powerful means of topping up your super!

One couple I worked with had decided to do exactly that. We sat down to devise a strategy for them, which was to use the equity in their home to pay for the deposits on some properties. With this approach, 80 to 90 per cent of the property would always be financed by loans secured by that property, while the equity in their home would be used to pay the required 10 to 20 per cent deposit along with stamp duty, legal fees and other buying costs.

We also made sure that these properties would not get cross collateralised, so that if our clients decided to refinance or sell at some point, they would not be stuck with a complicated financial structure that bunched their properties together.

Together, we had come up with a figure for what they needed for retirement, which was attainable with the capital from five investment properties. Even though they had the capacity to buy five properties straight away, because they had never invested before, they only wanted to buy one property at a time.

So they invested in the first one. They were very happy with that property and they found a tenant straight away. This gave them the confidence to move forward with their second rental property... and a third, and a fourth, and finally the fifth property.

In the end, it only took them about three years to get to their target of five properties. They are now sitting on a solid property portfolio that delivers a strong cash flow; they are just waiting for retirement, knowing that their income will be supplemented by their real estate assets.

The strategy we created for that couple was simple, clear and easy. It has worked for a number of our clients, because many of them have similar circumstances. The key here is to ensure that the experience is stress-free.

It can be very stressful when you are just starting out and you are navigating it all on your own; often, you can experience challenges before you have even got tenants in the house. Maybe your bank has issued you with the wrong loan documents or there is a delay in the registration of the property. There could be some problems picked up in the building and pest report or there may be a lot of bad weather that is delaying construction if you are building.

During these times, you need to be resilient. This is not always easy to do if you are investing on your own and people sometimes get discouraged if things do not go 100 per cent to plan. It is important to remember that these things happen, but with the right support, you can navigate these problems with less stress. When working with our clients, our goal is to make it as stress-free as possible for them by creating a strategy that will help cope with any problems, should they arise.

Decision-making based on dollars and sense

I have made the point several times that investing in property is a numbers game and that you need to focus on the facts and keep emotion out of the equation. However, there is a flip side of that coin that needs to be considered. There is a psychology to investing that involves your mindset and how you approach your money. Your attitude in this respect will have a huge impact on your overall success, because while you are making decisions based on the numbers, you also need to feel good about where you are now and where you are headed.

For instance, let's say you are renting your home right now. Depending on your circumstances, it may make much more sense from a financial point of view for you to continue renting while you invest in property. We often see this scenario with our clients, where it is the smarter decision – purely in financial terms – for a client to build wealth through property investment rather than buying their own home.

That said, we understand that making money is not the only thing that drives people. I have clients who, even though they completely understand the financial impacts, prefer the security of having a home rather than (or as well as) a property portfolio. For whatever reason, they desire the security and stability of their own home, even though they know this may come at a financial cost down the track.

This is absolutely fine. Sometimes, you have to recognise pure financial gain is not always the top priority and that the security of working towards owning your own home may be more important.

Whatever your decision, it is essential that you make it from an informed place. In this respect, investors must become really diligent in gathering information themselves from a wide variety of sources.

For example, if someone gives you a recommendation to buy a property in a particular suburb or town, you need to check the validity of that advice for yourself. Does your own research support this person's claim? If so, then you can proceed with confidence. However, moving forward on a property deal purely because someone has advised you to is a risky way to invest.

I advise my investor clients to talk to as many people as possible before they make up their mind on a property. Everybody has a different point of view and many of them will be quite valuable. Ultimately, you need to make up your own mind and the best way to do this is from an informed position.

There are many resources available that can help you check the advice you have been given. We are lucky today when compared to investors of the past, because the main sources are readily available on the internet. Here is a list of just some of the resources I recommend consulting:

- Corelogic – www.corelogic.com.au
- Residex – www.residex.com.au
- OnTheHouse – www.OnTheHouse.com.au
- BIS Shrapnel – www.bis.com.au

- SQM Research – www.sqmresearch.com.au
- Herron Todd White – www.htw.com.au
- Real Estate Investar – www.realestateinvestar.com.au

Sometimes you will have to pay to access in-depth statistics and information, but this is generally a small price to pay for the confidence you will gain that you are doing the right thing. It is important that you do your own research and talk to knowledgeable people. As you work through these different resources, you will work out quickly which advice makes sense and which does not make sense.

Quite often, all the investment advice you require can be found in the resources I have just mentioned. But good property investment decisions can also be made with the help of a bit of local knowledge. For example, if we can see that someone is developing a small estate in an area, we might start looking at the suburb in more detail. We will fly up there and have a look around, we will talk to a lot of real estate agents and we will walk into a few shops and talk to the owners.

Talking to the locals makes good sense because at the end of the day, there is nothing quite like scoping the area and talking to the locals to reaffirm your position that an investment location stacks up.

One situation where a property might look good on paper, but actually is not so special at all, relates to the often quoted 'median' price. The median price is calculated by finding the mid-way point between the most expensive and the cheapest properties sold in an area over a certain period. The median price could be well outside the actual price of homes sold in that area, if the selling volume is low.

I know of one case where a regional suburb in New South

Wales suddenly became the biggest and best growth area in Australia. It turns out that in this particular area, very few sales were recorded each year. So when a foreign buyer came in and bought a house for $1.2 million in this suburb where properties never sell for more than $600,000, the data was skewed considerably. Suddenly, the median went from $600,000 to $900,000, all because one property was purchased for $1.2 million.

This story demonstrates that numbers are great but they need to be verified. When we are looking at suburbs, we must remember to look for a significant number of sales so we can find trends and confirm that the numbers are accurate.

At Multifocus Properties & Finance, our goal is to empower people to make their own investment decisions. As I have mentioned previously, sometimes I have clients approach me who want me to simply tell them where to buy. I could confidently do this but I do not like this approach. I want you to make investment decisions because you feel educated, empowered and confident that the facts and figures make sense, not simply because you trust me. Ultimately, it is your money, your life and your decision to make.

CHAPTER 12

Where to from here?

CREATING WEALTH THROUGH property investing is not hard but it can be complicated. Hopefully by now you are feeling optimistic about your property investing future and after reading the processes outlined in this book, you feel confident about taking your next step.

The main message I would love you to take away from these pages is that when you start investing in property, you need to begin with the end in mind. Know where the (ideal) finish line is. Have a clear idea of where you are going. Only then can you discover how it all works and how the numbers click together, so you can put a plan in place to reach your goals.

Once people have an understanding of the structure and strategy of investing, it is then simply a matter of going ahead with it. But it is not always that simple, is it?

There are emotions involved. If you are a low-risk person with a low-risk attitude, then just the thought of taking tens of thousands of dollars out of your bank account to hand over for a property may have you breaking out in a sweat.

For these types of people, having a property coach or adviser can be invaluable. At Multifocus Properties & Finance, I counsel people through the process of property investing every day. I help them understand how it works, what the risks are and how to minimise the risks of losing money. As I have mentioned before, one of the favourite parts of my job is when someone 'gets it'. It is like a light switch has been flicked on and they suddenly understand how to achieve financial abundance through property investing.

Of course, even after this switch has been flicked, it can still be a process to get your mind around the idea of putting your thoughts and plans into action and actually buying an investment property.

I get it – it can be scary. But do you know what is even scarier? Reaching your retirement age and realising you will have to survive on an income of a few hundred dollars a week.

Let's say you have reached this far in the book. You have read all of the steps involved in finding and buying proven property performers to help you grow your wealth. But then you put this book down… and you do not do anything. What are you risking by procrastinating for a few years?

First of all, if you are reading this book then that means you are interested in property and you want to do something different with your life. You want to have that financial edge and step out from the mundane and the ordinary.

Looking ahead, you want to be able to retire comfortably and create a better life for yourself and your loved ones. If that is your intention, then at some point you have got to back yourself and say: 'I have enough knowledge. I have enough education. I have done enough research. Now, I need to actually do something.'

The big risk of waiting

For many people, they find comfort in the 'planning' stage. It is similar to going on a diet – or at least, planning to go on a diet. You feel confident that you are planning to make positive changes and excited about the potential outcome. But when it comes time to actually implement changes, you resist, because you are comfortable where you are.

Here is the risk you face: if your property planning phase keeps on going indefinitely, then you enter a procrastination phase – which is pretty much a phase where you do not go anywhere. You find more and more excuses not to do anything and then you complain that you have not got ahead in life.

One day, you look back and realise five years have gone past… then 10 years… and you still have not invested in property or moved your wealth forward.

I will hear from clients every now and then who say, 'Remember that property you recommended and I did not go through with it? I have looked into it and I can see that area has gone ahead – what is that property worth now?'

I will be the one to break the bad news that, yes, it is a strongly performing property, and in fact it has gone up in value by around $120,000 in the last few years… building someone else's wealth!

Without fail, they always say, 'I wish I had just bought it'.

Here is the thing: it is never too late. There is always an opportunity somewhere.

But the longer you wait, the less leverage you get and the less profitable it is for you. At some point you have to jump in and just do it.

The classic excuse that people make is, 'Well, what happens if I lose my job?' Funnily enough, that was my main reservation when I started investing in property myself. I was building quite a large portfolio and I worried about what would happen if I had 10 properties and lost my job. 'I would be stuffed,' I thought.

Then an accountant who worked for me said, 'If you lose your job and you do not own any properties, you are stuffed anyway!'

That was my light bulb moment. It made me realise that if I procrastinate because of all the disasters and eventualities that could happen, I will never do anything. You just have to do it.

I quickly realised that losing my job would not be the end of the world. How many people lose their job and go on to never, ever find another one? For most people, the reality is that when they lose their job, they can redeploy their skills and experience into another job within a couple of months.

Whether you own properties or not, you are going to have to find a way to pay your bills for those few months. Fortunately, you will still have rental income flowing in, so you will not fall behind in your mortgages. And, if you have put risk mitigation strategies in place (such as a financial buffer to deal with emergencies) then you should survive a job loss situation without too many bumps and bruises.

This is all psychological. If you are scared or uncomfortable about doing something different, you will be amazed at how clever you become at finding all sorts of excuses not to go ahead. But you have to overcome this and take it seriously. When I meet with new clients, I consider it a big part of my job to help them move past any negativity and overcome any procrastination.

In my experience, procrastination always leads to regret. It is something that people have to fight very hard to move past and it is not uncommon for me to hear people say, 'I have been looking at property for 10 years and I have never bought anything and now I regret it because I could have made so much more money.'

The reality is: if you do not risk anything, you are not going to get anywhere.

If you do not do something, nothing will happen.

If you do not take action towards getting rich, you will never get rich.

So now, it is time to take action.

How to move past fear and grow your wealth

Without a doubt, fear is the main reason why people procrastinate. The sad fact is, however, that a lot of the time their fear is unfounded, because just talking to someone could help them to work it all out.

Working with trusted, experienced professionals will help to give you the confidence that you are on the right track. This means creating a strong team to assist you, which should include:

- A property adviser, to ensure you invest with confidence in quality properties that will grow in value and build your wealth.
- A mortgage broker, to guide you towards the right financial structures and loan products.
- An accountant, to help you minimise your tax and maximise the amount of money you make (and keep!) each year.
- A financial planner, who can help paint a picture of a profitable retirement and show you how to plug the gap between where you are now and where you are headed.

These first two professional services are ones that we offer at Multifocus Properties & Finance. When we meet a new client, we sit down with them and actually tailor the generalities that are set out in this book to their personal financial circumstances and goals. Working together, we create an investment property strategy that fits with their financial profile and their goals.

We consider it our job to hold our clients by the hand, all the way to the end, from the very first property onwards; we essentially offer support and guidance for life!

We build relationships with our clients because we want to be part of their success. As such, it is in our interests to provide exceptional service so that our clients will keep coming back. We are not interested in selling one property or setting up one loan structure and then moving on; rather, we want to share our knowledge and help people be as successful as they can be.

Take research, for instance: I have someone in my staff whose full-time role is dedicated purely to research. He looks into locations, studies economic growth, conducts due diligence on market trends, vacancy rates, rental growth and more. From his initial research he locates an area and then narrows down the type of property we should be trying to find for our clients, whether it is an apartment, a house or townhouse, to best suit the market.

Then we drill down further to find properties to fit our clients' individual strategies. We look at the numbers on every property and every time we present a property to a client, it has got a 10-year projection attached to it, so they can see what the cash flow is, how much tax they are getting back and how much rent they are expected to earn from that property.

This is the level of detail that we go to, to ensure that we can find our clients good quality properties with good capital growth – because after all, that is the name of the game! It is also essential that you manage cash flow while you own your property, which is why we calculate the cash flow projection of properties to ensure it fits your circumstances.

The reason we invest so much time and so many resources into researching on behalf of our clients is because we know the fears that can keep them up at night – we have been there ourselves!

There are many things you can start to worry about as a landlord such as how will you find a tenant? What will happen if the tenant damages the property? How will you manage mortgage repayments if you have a vacancy period? These things can lead you to procrastinate even longer, as you become so fearful about the potential issues that could arise when investing in property.

The truth is, no problem is insurmountable.

To find a tenant, make sure you buy property in a popular, central location that appeals to tenants. Then make sure you use a good property manager to manage it and to manage your tenants.

If the tenant damages the property, your property manager will evict the tenant if necessary and find a new tenant. Then, you can lodge an insurance claim with your landlord insurance provider to recover the costs of the repairs.

To manage your mortgage repayments, if you have a vacancy period, you might have to draw on your savings or equity, which you have earmarked as an emergency buffer to deal with exactly these situations.

We walk our clients through all of these potential scenarios to help them get comfortable with them before they happen. Just as importantly, we help them to come up with solutions and exit strategies in advance.

Of course, you do not need a property adviser in order to successfully invest in real estate and create your own wealth. For some people, building their own knowledge base and learning about ideal strategies gives them everything they need to confidently move forward and start accumulating property.

For others it takes a little more guidance, which is where we come in. If you have a low threshold for risk, or you are not sure what to do next, or you just realise that property investing is not what you do best, then I would strongly encourage you to reach out to an experienced, qualified property adviser as your next step.

By working together, you can address your fears, minimise any risks, and gain the confidence to charge purposefully forward towards achieving your wealth goals.

INDEX

accountant 52, 65, 69, 75, 92, 150, 178-179
accumulation phase 18, 81-109
acquisition strategy 5, 58
active investing 72, 153
aggressive buying strategy 92-94
ANZ 34, 36
asset, illiquid 6
assets 75
Australian capital cities 113-114
Australian Prudential Regulation Authority (APRA) 24, 126
Australian Securities and Investments Commission (ASIC) 8

balance 98, 104-105
bank advice 42-43
banks 47-49, 72
BIS Shrapnel 172
body corporate 13
borrowing capacity 23, 26-27, 37-38, 44-45, 72-73, 90
borrowing power 26
boundaries 72-74, 76
building and pest inspection 29, 170

buyer's agent 7, 61
capacity 22, 25, 72
capital 22-23
capital gains 91-92, 94
capital gains tax (CGT) 4, 59-60
capital growth 45, 59, 94-96, 98, 104, 127, 149, 168, 180
capital growth, long-term 108-109, 114
car loan 26
career history 32-33
cash flow 45, 57-58, 60, 72, 124, 139, 167-168, 170, 180
cash flow, balance 94-96, 104-105
cash flow, investor 103
cash flow, negative 45, 105, 124
cash flow, positive 13, 83, 94-95
Channel 9 88
Charters Towers 50
commercial real estate 144-145
Commonwealth Bank (CBA) 24
consolidation 163-174
conveyancer 29, 69
CoreLogic 4, 98, 172
credit card 26-27, 35
credit file 34-39, 127

credit record 34-35, 48
credit risk 125-126
cross collateralising 49-51
customer loyalty 40-41

debt 23, 25-30, 45, 72-73
debt, bad 91, 127
decision-making 171-174
deposit 25, 28-30, 56-57, 72, 92
depreciation 102-103, 134-138
depreciation schedule 29
development project 70, 73
diversify 77, 79, 93, 119, 141
do-it-yourself (DIY) 63, 68
drawdown phase 59, 147-182
due diligence 3, 57, 105, 109, 118, 120 152, 180

economy 31, 99
economy, local 63
economy, strong 99, 128
education 54-66, 69, 163-174
emotions 62, 89, 121, 175
equity 27, 48, 72, 75, 79, 90, 113, 181
equity advantage 90-91
equity, redraw 51
expenses 42

fear 179-182
fees, building and pest inspection 29
fees, conveyancing 29
fees, finance and loan application 29
finance 21-53, 54, 169

finance broker 52-53
Finance Brokers Association of Australia (FBAA) 52
financial buffers 79, 127, 178, 181
financial limits 64, 73
financial opportunities 64
financial planner 75, 87, 92, 150, 179
financial structure 75-76, 170
first-time investors 68-70, 92, 163
fundamentals, property selection 97
funding sources 58

get-rich-quick scheme 65-66
goals, property 70, 153, 161, 175
Global Financial Crisis (GFC) 36, 44, 64
Greenwood, Ross 88
growth stage 59

Herron Todd White 105, 173
home loan 27, 42, 48, 91
loan, no doc 45
Household Expenditure Measure (HEM) 26
hybrid solution 60

illiquid asset 6
income 25-32, 37, 58
income potential, long-term 30
income protection insurance 65
income, over-estimating 41-42
individualised approach 8-9

INDEX

inflation 18
infrastructure 98, 100-101, 127
insurance 65, 134
insurance, life 65
interest payable 76
interest rates 45-46, 58, 105, 123, 140
invest, wrong way to 132-145
investing phase 91
investment property loan 51
investing risks 76-78, 117-131
investing without professional support 165-166
investment goals 72, 180
investment strategies to avoid 133-134
investment strategy, four key pillars 71-76
investment strategy, long-term 90
investment strategy, value of a good 168-171
investment, long-term 107
investments, passive 63, 103, 113, 151
investors, couple 74
investors, single 70
investors, first-time 68-70, 92

job status 30-32
joint partnership 142-144
joint venture 74, 93, 142-144

landlord 65, 113, 129, 132-133, 144-145, 163

landlord's insurance 130, 181
Lawless, Tim 98
legal fees 169
legal framework 74-75
lenders 43, 72
Lenders Mortgage Insurance (LMI) 28-30, 32, 56-57, 139
lending criteria 22-24, 36, 43
lifestyle 7, 63-64, 88, 99, 151, 152, 159
line of credit 76, 79
liquidating 60
liquidity risk 120-121
loan application 25, 32, 43, 48
loan criteria 41
loan to value ratio (LVR) 28, 32-33, 45, 48-50, 57-58, 126, 145
loan, risk 29
loans, pay down 60, 155-156
location 77-79, 97-99, 129, 169, 180
location hunting 100
long-term investment 107
low-leverage properties 133-135

maintenance costs, lower 134
market cycle 79, 98, 105-107, 118, 127
market performance 99
market risk 118
Medicare Levy Surcharge 103, 136
Mercedes 21
mining town 64, 77-78, 94, 141-142

185

Mortgage & Finance Association of Australia (MFAA) 52
mortgage 24, 29, 42, 91, 113, 124, 178
mortgage broker 33, 43, 47-49, 51-53, 69, 73, 102, 179
mortgage market 40
mortgage repayments 45, 181
mortgage repayments, making extra 153-154
Multifocus Properties & Finance 6, 9, 58, 71, 149, 174-175, 179

negative cash flow 45, 105, 124
negative equity situation 141
negative gearing 3-6, 17, 95, 102, 136
negative reporting 34
no doc loan 45

objectives 71-72
offset account 51, 62, 76
OnTheHouse 172
ownership structure 74-75

passive buying strategy 92-94
passive investments 63, 103, 113, 151
pension 71
personal loan 26, 36
phase, accumulation 18, 83
phase, drawdown 59, 147-182
phase, investing 91
phase, planning 18, 58-59, 131, 177
phase, transition 59-60, 111-145

planning 17-79, 177
planning phase 18, 58-59, 131, 177
point of difference 98, 108-109
poor investments 133-145
population growth 63, 98, 127
portfolio, designing 85-96
portfolio, selling 59-60, 157-159
positive cash flow 13, 83, 94-95
positive gearing 46
positive reporting 34
price appreciation risk 127-128
procrastination risk 130-131, 177-178
properties, over-committing 139-141
property adviser 69, 150, 179
property buying costs 29, 56, 169
property clock 107
property condition 98, 101-102
property cycle 105-108
property experts 7
property goals 70, 153, 161, 175
property investing, key elements 61-66
property investing, strategy 5, 58, 64, 67-79
property investment decisions 63-64, 77
property investments, purpose 86-89
property manager 12, 102, 109, 113, 130

INDEX

property portfolio, planning 17-79
property, choosing the right 97-109
proven property performer 83-84, 97, 176
Real Estate Institute of Australian (REIA) 113
Real Estate Investar 173
refinance 41, 48, 50
renovation 76-77, 104, 138
rental income 43, 57, 76, 91, 96, 98, 155-156
rental yield 13, 106, 135, 139, 145, 167
repayments, interest-only 45
research 64
Reserve Bank of Australia (RBA) 123
Residex 172
retirement 59-60, 71, 84, 86-89, 92, 151-162, 164, 176
retirement age 152
retirement, lifestyle 152
retirement, real estate-funded 161-162
risk 30, 45-46, 72, 76-78
– management 46-47, 65
– management plan 65
– mitigation strategy 119-131, 161
– profile 33, 64, 72, 84, 93, 149
– credit 125-126
– interest rate 123
– liquidity 120-121
– market 118
– minimising 96
– price appreciation 127-128
– procrastination 130-131, 177-178
– strategy 121-122
– tenancy 129
rule of one thousand 57, 96, 100, 105, 139

salary sacrifice 87
savings account 56, 60, 65
savings plan 38
security 22
self-employed 30-32, 42, 47
selling 59-60, 157-159
serviceability 48, 74
set and forget 102, 135
shares 6
SQM Research 173
stamp duty 4, 28-29, 56, 120, 154, 169
strategy 25, 28, 30, 32, 34, 70
– advice 42-43
– risk 121-122
– acquisition 5
– aggressive buying 92-94
– passive buying 92-94
– property investing 5, 58, 64, 67-79, 101
– risk mitigation 119-131, 161
superannuation 71, 86-89, 93, 157, 169
supply and demand 106, 109

tax 51-52, 58, 74, 95, 120
tax concessions 4-5
tax deductions 75, 91, 102
tax rebate 58
tax return 42
Telstra 34
tenancy risk 129
tenant population 63
tenants 11-12, 62, 77, 108, 128, 139, 145, 165, 170, 181

theory 89
time in the market 89-90, 92, 169
transition phase 59-60, 111-145
transition strategy 154-162
trial and error, learning 166-168

vacancy rate 108, 180
value 85
VEDA Advantage 36

multifocus
Properties & Finance

1300 266 350
www.multifocus.com.au

Printed by Libri Plureos GmbH in Hamburg, Germany